VANITY PRESS
&
THE PROPER POET

by

Johnathon Cli

Typeset and Published
by
The Author
27 Mill Road
Fareham
Hampshire
Tel: 0329 822218

Printed by
Meon Valley Printers
Bishops Waltham (0489 895460)

© Johnathon Clifford 1994

Cover designed by the author

Previous publications by the same author:

Some Vast And Hideous Army (1987).
Metric Feet & Other Gang Members (1993).

ISBN   0 9522503 5 7

Dedicated

To the Rosemary Arthurs of this world who
give unselfishly in support of poetry book
publication, and to all those who work towards
the day when there will be no-one trying to
'make a fast buck' from the innocent and
unwary aspiring poet.

ACKNOWLEDGEMENTS

I must first thank Barry Turner and his team for *The Writer's Handbook*. Some of the initial spade–work for this book was done with the WH almost constantly on my knee, propped up in eye's view, or within easy page–turning distance. The sheer effort of collecting together the basic information needed would surely have proved too Herculean a task to even start – but for the WH's clarity of indexing.

Then I must thank Richard Bell who was kind enough to give his editorial opinion and advice on my approach to my subject, and to Kate Pool of the Society of Authors who sent me (along with invaluable advice) a very helpful pamphlet. Thanks also to Ruth Gladwin of Stephens Innocent (Solicitors) who, feeling so strongly about the vanity press, gave me all the free advice she could afford.

To Peggy Poole for her chapter on Women's self–perceived need to be separate in the book publishing world.

To all the publishers, bookshops, arts associations, and everyone else who so readily gave me the information I required.

To the gentleman who was kind enough to give me his permission to use his poems.

To the two who, by allowing 'Roberts' and 'Locke' the use of their homes as accommodation addresses, helped make Chapter III possible.

To Helen Robinson for her overseeing, proof–reading and, above all, forbearance.

And of course to David Archard and crew at Meon Valley Printers, who once again helped make my pease–pottage of a book have more the aroma of cordon bleu cookery!

My gratitude and thanks to you all . . .

CONTENTS

Chapter V

Chapter VI

NB. *All adverts that appear in this book do so free of charge as I feel each to be of value to the poet.*

* * *

INTRODUCTION

Many people had kept telling me I ought to write a book about vanity press, but personally I felt it to be more like yesterday's news – stale and boring – than something that would really interest anyone today. But still the requests came in . . .

It was the fantastic response to my *Metric Feet & Other Gang Members* that made me feel I should write a second book (certainly not in my mind to do so when writing the 'one–off' Metric Feets!). For a few people to say how much they had enjoyed it was one thing; to have so many people saying it gave me the confidence that I perhaps had something worthwhile to say and an interesting style in which to say it. But how? I mean . . . to simply write a book about vanity publishers would be boring. Write a book about publishing in general? For any company to risk publishing a poetry book necessitates a market . . . include the bookshops as well? While I'm at it, how about adding those who so often make it possible – those who give grants, awards and prizes for poetry books?

Giving so much detail of each publisher, each bookshop, each grant making body, freeze–frames them all at this moment of writing – March 1994 – but I can see no real problem with that, for although the minutiae of detail will change in the months and years ahead, the overall intent, attitude and general approach will remain much the same. So freeze–framing is valid. It gives you an overall 'feel' for how each operates, how their management looks on poetry and the poetry book.

Where the vanity press is concerned: What is it? Who is it? I can only list the characters in the drama – be both defence and prosecution lawyer. You, reader, the only one who may be both judge and jury.

CHAPTER I

However often you have the odd poem published – odd in the sense of 'spasmodically amongst the interminable rejection slips' rather than odd in the sense of 'weird' – it does little toward your becoming the recognised poet whose poetry is sought in every bookshop and loudly on everyone's lips, the unobtainable dream for all but the minutest number of aspiring poets.

No, the only achievement that moves you, however arthritically and haltingly, in that direction is to have a book of your own poetry published. That is what this book is all about. The how and where, the who (and who not), of getting your own book funded, published and sold.

Some would argue that the only poets worthy of publication are the few who live in the rarified atmosphere of the Establishment. The difficulty of getting into that strange world would seem to have much in common with the most contorted of Masonic rituals. But don't worry, being accepted by such is as much the toss of a dice as anything. The being in the right place at the right time. The knowing the right person or people and sometimes, being a poet of real and genuine talent. Not being accepted by the establishment could well prove (in the long run) beneficial.

Consider: during the last two decades of the 19th century there was a marked increase in the publication of poetry, but what the equivalent to today's Establishment forecast would be the poetry to last – didn't. What it was inclined to pooh–pooh – has. Those who liked to think themselves a cut above the rest in literary flair and ability put down more good poets than they managed to praise.

Instead of an Establishment in today's sense, there was the *Yellow Book*. Instigated by Aubrey Beardsley and Henry Harland in January 1894 and published by John

Lane it was to have, according to its innovators, a single raison d'être – that of excellence.

At that time some great English poets were writing. Rudyard Kipling, who these 'critics' didn't think a poet of any standing, A E Housman who was belittled by them, and Thomas Hardy who had to wait years before he was able to get his first book of verse published and then the critics didn't like it! Robert Bridges had to publish most of his work privately as he received so little acceptance from these self-elected custodians of excellence. But most of the work featured by the *Yellow Book* has long since vanished almost without trace.

So you see, you may well be the most brilliant of poets yet still find the Establishment will give you little credence. Let it worry you not one jot!

What then is important where the publication of poetry is concerned? We need to capture and retain the best of what is being written today – that goes without saying – but what else? My theory is that poetry is rather like painting or playing the piano. Practise painting techniques for long enough and you may become proficient enough to hold a public exhibition from which you may well sell paintings and give those who both view and buy them a great deal of pleasure. Practise scales and arpeggios until they come out of your ears and you may well become a good enough pianist to give public performances, which again will share a deal of pleasure with an undefined number of people. So it is with poetry. Practise your art and your poetry may reach a standard which warrants publication.

None of this of course can make you the brilliant pianist, painter or poet. That cannot be taught, that has to be there from the start, and that brings me to my 'Journeyman Poet'. He who quietly and in his own backyard beavers away at his poetry year in, year out. He who is the back

THE ALDEBURGH POETRY FESTIVAL PRIZE
(FOR A FIRST COLLECTION)

This annual prize, sponsored jointly by the Aldeburgh Bookshop and Waterstones & Co, is awarded for a first collection of at least 40 poems *published* in Great Britain or Eire.

The prize is currently worth £500 and comes with an invitation to read at the Festival the following year.

Submissions are welcome either from publishers or from individual poets.

For the purpose of the prize the year runs from October 1st to September 30th.

Entries – 2 bound or proof copies with a note of the publication date – should be sent before October 1st to: The Aldeburgh Poetry Festival Prize, Newby House, 40 Cumberland Street, Woodbridge, Suffolk IP12 4AD.

* * *

bone of the small presses and magazines in that it is he who is everyone's subscriber. The poet who is indeed the majority of us. Not the brilliant poet but, as the amateur and aspiring pianist or painter deserves his public performance and exhibition, so this poet deserves publication of a book as much as the most highly prized and nationally acclaimed of poets. Remember . . . what we praise today may well be forgotten tomorrow, and vice versa.

If you are to succeed in getting a manuscript accepted for publication you first need to know who the publishers are. So I searched out every name and address of those listed as publishers of poetry in *The Writer's Handbook* and other recognised reference manuals and wrote to each asking them to give me a basic breakdown of how they worked. I also did the same with a list of minority and ethnic group publishers supplied by the Poetry Library at the South Bank complex in London, and here is what I found.

UK Poetry Book Publishers

A.

Patricia Oxley, Editor of **Acumen**, 6 The Mount, Higher Furzeham, Brixham, South Devon TQ5 8QY tel: 0803 851098, tells me that ideally they would like to publish about 4 books a year but at present are only able to produce 1. This is often by invitation or through the *Acumen* magazine. No royalties are paid, but there is either a one-off payment or a large number of free copies, plus copies at cost. Marketing is via a launch, flyers, readings and most important, repping of bookshops. Poets are advised to see the sort of material the press already publishes before submitting their own work.

For **Anchor Books** – see Forward Press

THE ROSEMARY ARTHUR AWARD 1989

This annual award is for a first collection of poetry only. To be eligible a poet must not previously have had a book published, nor self-published a book.

Before December 31st a poet must submit 40 poems together with a £5 reading fee and a suitable sae for the return of the work and notification of the winner to: The Administrators, 27 Mill Rd, Fareham, Hants PO16 0TH tel: 0329 822218.

The Trustees of the National Poetry Foundation select a short list of six entries and, having removed any means of identifying the author, send these six collections on to Rosemary Arthur who on February 3rd each year (her birthday) announces the winner.

The prize consists of a cash prize of £100, an engraved brass and glass carriage clock (worth some £60 at 1994 prices) and the publication of the winner's book.

Rosemary Arthur has covenanted £1,000 a year during her lifetime for this award and made provision in her will for its continuance into the foreseeable future.

Winners so far:

1990	Robert Roberts	*Amphibious Landings*
1991	David Lightfoot	*Down Private Lanes*
1992	Judith Wright	*Through Broken Glass*
1993	Val Moore	*Fledgling Confidence*
1994	Sheila Simmons	*Take The Long View*

This year (1994) the runner-up, Barbara Balch, also had her book *After The Storm* published.

For **Andre Deutsch Ltd** – see Deutsch

Editorial Directors Peter Jay and Julia Sterland for **Anvil Press Poetry**, 69 King George Street, London SE10 8PX tel: 081 858 2946, say they publish on average 12 books a year. They decide who to publish simply "on merit." Normally pay a 10% royalty though that is dependent on the particular contract. They have no easily definable marketing policy. Anyone may submit a manuscript, with an sae.

For **Arrival Press** – see Forward Press

B.

Dave Cunliffe for **BB Books**, Spring Bank, Longsight Road, Copster Green, Blackburn, Lancs BB1 9EU tel: 0254 249128, writes that although they no longer undertake printing for self-publishers they will still do the typesetting. This works out at £2 to £3 per A5 poetry page and £10 per 1,000 words for prose. BB Books does still publish an average of 4 books a year, pays no royalties and markets the books through adverts, leaflets and reviews. Unsolicited work may be submitted with an sae.

For **Blackie** – see Penguin.

Director and Editorial Head Anne Tannahill for **Blackstaff Press**, 3 Galway Park, Dundonald, Belfast BT16 0AN tel: 0232 487161, writes that they publish an average of 2 books a year. They choose what to publish on a basis of a combination of personal taste and market considerations. They pay standard royalties of around 7½% of the retail price of each copy sold. They market their books through advertising, mail shots, catalogues, sales cards, reviews, features and readings. Anyone may submit a manuscript but Blackstaff do receive far more than they can publish and therefore some delay in receiving an answer should be expected. They mainly, but not exclusively, publish Irish poetry.

Simon Thisk, Chairman of **Bloodaxe Books**, P O Box 1SN, Newcastle Upon Tyne NE99 1SN tel: 091 232 5988, tells me they publish an average of 50 books a year. They select work on "literary quality," pay a 10% royalty and market their books through bookshop repping, press publicity, direct mail and overseas distribution. He would recommend Paul Hyland's *Getting Into Poetry* (published by Bloodaxe) to anyone thinking of trying to get published and says anyone may submit a manuscript to them with sae.

Jessica Huntley for **Bogle L'Overture**, 141 Coldershaw Road, London W13 9DU tel: 081 579 4920, says they publish 2 books a year that are mainly anti-racist, positive image, relative to African/Caribbean, progressive Third World themes. Royalties are 7½ to 10%. Marketing is through distributors. Unsolicited manuscripts may be submitted with an sae.

Margaret Tims, General Editor for **Brentham Press**, 40 Oswald Road, St. Albans, Herts tel: 0727 835731, writes that they publish on average 4 books a year including one volume of *Poet's England*. Collections are normally accepted through personal knowledge of the author and over the last few years most have been members of the Ver Poets poetry group. It is stipulated that individual poets guarantee to take a specified number of copies of their book (usually 100) to be supplied 'at trade'. In theory a 10% royalty is paid when half the edition is sold, or costs covered. In practice, when authors take a bulk supply (on which they make a profit) no royalty is paid on copies sold by the publisher. Where marketing is concerned poets are encouraged to arrange readings in their own area for which publicity material is supplied, selected review copies and circulars to relevant trade outlets and book fairs are sent out. *Poet's England* is promoted by circulars to all bookshops in the country, advance information to wholesalers and library suppliers, review copies mainly to the local press. Unsolicited work is never accepted and a preliminary letter (with sae) should always be sent.

For **British Haiku Society** – see Haiku

Catherine Mason, writing for **Broadcast Books**, 4 Cotham Vale, Bristol BS6 6HR tel: 0272 732010, says that they only publish 1 or 2 publications a year and encourage the revival of old poetry rather than new writers – (*author's note:* the delightful, detailed and magical *The Story Of Poetry* being a prime example). They publish on merit and might on occasions suggest an author underwrite a part of the publication costs. Royalties would be paid at 10% or 15% of net receipts. Marketing is in the form of mailings, review copies, repping and a modest bookshop launch. No unsolicited material.

For **Businesslike Publishing**, 'Burnside', Station Road, Beauly, Inverness shire IV4 7EQ tel: 0463 782258, Iain R McIntyre says that he publishes 2 or 3 books a year but is very dependent on The Society of Civil Service Authors for what he does. He says that he "publishes on a vanity basis – charging what it costs. In fact a printing fee with nothing added. In fact, people are getting their books before being asked to pay anything." Unsolicited poets? "Not really, I usually write back and tell them it is hard to make money from poetry and regretfully turn them down."

THE CHOLMONDELEY AWARDS FOR POETS

The Cholmondeley Awards for Poets were founded by the late Dowager Marchioness of Cholmondeley in 1966 to recognise the achievement and distinction of individual poets. It is not a competition award and submissions are not required. The recipients are chosen by the Awards Committee for their general body of work and contribution to poetry.

The Society of Authors
84 Drayton Gardens
London
SW10 9SB
071 373 6642
Fax 071 373 5768

C.

Chairman, Managing Director and Editor, John Calder of **Calder Publications Ltd**, 9–15 Neal Street, London WC2H 9TU tel: 071 497 1741, writes that they publish one book a year, pay a 10% royalty, market the book through reviews, bookshops and poetry readings and that unsolicited work *may not* be submitted.

Tony Seddon, Director of Education at the **Cambridge University Press**, The Edinburgh Building, Shaftesbury Road, Cambridge CB2 2RU tel: 0223 315052, explained that they publish some 7 poetry books a year which come under the responsibility of Keith Rose, Editor of Secondary English, and that they will be publishing Stage 1 of *Cambridge Reading* in January 1996 with Stage 2 in 1997. There are to be 10 poetry books in this scheme which is for pupils between the ages of 5–11. Royalties are confidential. Marketing through catalogues, leaflets, sales teams in schools, adverts and overseas agents. Doesn't really seem suitable for unsolicited work.

For **Canongate Press Ltd**, 14 Frederick Street, Edinburgh, Scotland EH2 2HG tel: 031 220 3800, Fiona Morrison on behalf of the Founder, Stephanie Wolfe Murray, told me they will consider poetry from anywhere in the UK, not just Scottish poets. They publish 2 or 3 books a year which are chosen for their "quality as adult literary poetry." They pay advances which are variable and "normal royalties." Marketing is through their own publicity department. Unsolicited manuscripts welcome with sae.

Robin Robertson, Senior Editoral Director for **Jonathan Cape**, 20 Vauxhall Bridge Road, London SW1V 2SA tel: 071 973 9730, writes that he re-launched the Cape poetry list in April 1994 and expects to publish between 4 and 6 books a year. Choice will be solely on "excellence of writing." Royalties are 10% of published price. Marketing of any book depends on a number of unique characteristics and he didn't feel able to generalise. Unsolicited manuscripts are welcome but *must be accompanied by return postage.*

Michael Schmidt, Managing and Editorial Director for the **Carcanet Press Ltd,** 208 Corn Exchange Buildings, Manchester M4 3BQ tel: 061 834 8730, rang me to say that they published 25 poets last year and this year will be including 8 first collections in their list. The poets chosen are those whose work appeals to Michael directly and he publishes work not only by English poets, but also those from Europe, the Commonwealth and America. Where royalties are concerned Carcanet pay 10% hardback and 7½% paperback, with advances of between £300 and £2,000 – each book is individual, as is the marketing of that book, and no hard and fast rules can apply. Unsolicited work is encouraged only from those who *first read Carcanet's catalogue and publications.* Submitting on the off–chance of acceptance is simply a waste of everyone's time and should not be attempted.

For **Kyle Cathie** – see Kyle

Sarah Holloway for **Chatto & Windus Ltd,** Random House, 20 Vauxhall Bridge Road, London SW1V 2SA tel: 071 233 6058, says they publish on average 5 or 6 books a year, chosen by their Poetry Editor, Simon Armitage. These may be books by new authors. Royalties are between 7½%–10% and an advance may be paid. Marketing is through their own in–house Publicity Manager. Unsolicited manuscripts may be sent with an sae.

Dr James Whetter for **CNP Publications,** Roseland, Gorran, St. Austell, Cornwall PL26 6MS tel: 0726 843501, reports that they produce a book every three years which is generated from their magazine *The Cornish Banner.* Work is only that with a Cornish or Celtic leaning and interest. Royalties are not paid. Marketing is not really necessary as those published are well-known in Cornwall. Poetry to do with Cornwall is welcome, with an sae.

For **Crabflower Pamphlets** – see Frogmore Press

J. Precious, Editor of the **Curlew Press,** Hare Cottage, Kettlesing, Harrogate, North Yorkshire HG3 2LB tel: 0423 770686, writes to say that he publishes on average 1 book a year, the work of which must be of "a high standard." He doesn't offer royalties and markets the book by sending out review copies. Unsolicited work may be submitted with an sae.

D.

From **Andre Deutsch Ltd,** 106 Great Russell Street, London WC1B 3LJ tel: 071 580 2746, Helen Fewster, Editorial Department, told me the last poetry book they had published was by John Hegley in 1992 and although they were involved in a reprint in 1994 of the best of Ogden Nash to be titled *I Wouldn't Have Missed It,* or *Candy Is Dandy*, they no longer publish poetry as it has proved not financially viable for them to do so.

For **Smith/Doorstop Books** – see Poetry Business Ltd

E.

On behalf of **Enitharmon Press,** 36 St. George's Avenue, London N7 0HD tel: 071 607 7194, Stephen Stuart–Smith writes to tell me that they publish 12 poets a year. All manuscripts are very carefully considered by the editor and by members of Enitharmon's board. In any year there are always books by poets who have an existing association with the press. They are also committed to fostering new talent and some of the best poets whose work is coming to the fore in magazines and journals are invited to submit their first collections for consideration. Royalties vary according to contract. Marketing is by review copies to leading newspapers and journals, readings, radio broadcasts and interviews and liaising closely with their representatives in the UK, Europe and the USA. Unsolicited work is *most definitely not* wanted.

For **Envoi Poets Publications**, 'Penffordd', Newport, Pembrokeshire, Dyfed, Wales SA42 0QT tel: 0239 820285, Anne Lewis–Smith tells me that she publishes between 10 and 14 books a year with the choice of poet being completely her own. Envoi asks the poets to subsidise their publication but all the monies from sales go to the poet. Her normal print run is 300 copies which she helps the poet market with in the region of 18 review copies. She says that she has published poets from as far afield as Canada, America, Germany and Switzerland, apart from those home–grown. She pointed out that although EPP doesn't make a profit it is important as an encouragement to the poet which, at a certain stage, is so often needed. Unsolicited manuscripts are welcome with an sae, but it must be noted that Envoi Publications is to cease accepting (or rejecting) books from December 1994.

F.

On behalf of **Faber & Faber Ltd**, 3 Queen Square, London WC1N 3AU tel: 071 465 0045, Jane Feaver, Assistant Poetry Editor, writes that they publish on average 4 new poets a year and between 10 and 15 established poets. Their poetry editor, Christopher Reid, chooses what he feels to be the "most excellent." Royalties are confidential and marketing through the normal channels of reviews, readings etc. It is presumed that unsolicited material may be submitted.

For **Fantail** – See **Penguin**.

The Rev John Waddington–Feather for **Feather Books**, 'Fair View', Old Coppice, Lyth Bank, Shrewsbury, Shropshire tel: 0743 872177, tells me they publish 2 books of religious poetry a year. Most books are for personal friends who pay for all the printing and advertising and any postage or telephone calls. The authors receive all but 10 copies of their book which are retained for "copyright reasons." Unsolicited poets may submit a small selection of religious poetry, with the usual sae.

Jacqueline Gonzalez–Marina, Founder of **Fern Publications**, 24 Frosty Hollow, East Hunsbury, Northamptonshire NN4 0SY tel: 0604 701730, tells me that she publishes an average of 2 books a year. Choice is dependent on quality and subject. Manuscripts often come through their magazine *Dandelion*. They also publish in English/French or English/Spanish translation. The poet pays for the book "at cost, which is usually between £3 and £5 a copy," Jacqueline says. Marketing is through magazines with whom she has a contact, newspapers and radio. Unsolicited material is welcome with an sae.

Peter Lewis for the **Flambard Press**, 4 Mitchell Avenue, Jesmond, Newcastle-Upon-Tyne NE2 3LA tel: 091 281 5196, writes that they publish an average of 7 poets (3 in one anthology for instance). An editorial board concentrates mainly on Northern poets. Royalties are 10% or a flat rate

THE GEOFFREY FABER MEMORIAL PRIZE

This prize is awarded alternately year on year for a poetry book and a book of prose fiction. It was established in 1963 as a memorial to the founder and first chairman of Faber & Faber.

For full details apply to:

The Geoffrey Faber Memorial Prize
Faber & Faber Ltd
3 Queen Square
London
WC1N 3AU
tel: 071 465 0045

* * *

equivalent to 10% and marketing is through Password. Unsolicited material may be submitted with an sae.

Forest Books of 20 Forest View, London E4 7AY tel: 081 529 8470, wrote that none of my questions were applicable as "we only publish poetry in translation."

Forward Press 1-2 Wainman Road, Woodston, Peterborough PE2 7BU tel: 0733 230746 (*no relation in any way to Forward Publishing of 5 Great Pulteney Street, London*) consists of several separate publications and publishing operations.

Michelle Abbott, Editor of **Anchor Books**, writes that they publish between 36 and 40 anthologies every year. The work is chosen by the editor and depends both on subject matter and approach. Royalties of 5% softback and 10% hardback are paid to charity, not to the authors. Unsolicited work may be submitted with an sae.

Trudi Ramm for the **Arrival Press** (same address but tel: 0733 230762), tells me she publishes around 36 anthologies a year and looks for traditional rhyming poetry with the intention of attracting "the man in the street." Royalties of 10% hardback and 5% softback are split between the poets featured. Marketing is by mail shot, review copies and local bookshops. Unsolicited manuscripts may be submitted with an sae, but no material "likely to prove offensive" will be accepted.

Ian Walton, Editor of **Poetry Now Publications**, writes that they published 14 anthologies and 3 individual books in 1993 but are hoping to increase that number. The work for the anthologies is chosen by an editorial panel; for an individual's book by himself or a partner. They pay royalties of 5% softback and 10% hardback and unsolicited submissions are welcome.

Andrew Head for the **Poetry Now Young Writers** tells

THE FORWARD PUBLISHING POETRY PRIZES

£10,000	Best	Individual Collection
£5,000	Best	First Collection
£1,000	Best	Individual Poem

Books and individual poems from a maximum of five poets may be submitted by publishers who are resident in the UK. Entries (6 copies) must be sent to Sandra Vince, Administrator, Book Trust, Book House, 45 East Hill, London SW18 2QZ tel: 081 870 9055 to arrive before 30th September.

Entries for the two 'Collection' categories must have been published between 1st August in the previous year and 30th September in the year of entry. Entries may be submitted in proof form if necessary.

Entries of single poems must have been published in an anthology/magazine between 1st August in the previous year and 30th June in year of entry. If the poem was the winner of a national competition, the result must have been declared between those dates.

The winners will be announced and prizes presented in October.

William Sieghart, Chairman of Forward Publishing, wrote on 27th October 1992, "one of the reasons why I wanted to revive what used be called the 'Guinness' was the way in which that particular prize brought poetry out of poetry corner. That's what we are trying to do. To give poetry a better focus rather than the rather disparate way in which it is promoted at the moment."

me that three times a year they circulate each and every school throughout the British Isles (over 3,000) inviting them to submit poems on behalf of their 11 to 17 year old pupils. This creates a competition situation from which Andrew Head and his manager Sarah Andrew choose the best poems submitted to form an anthology. From this anthology there is a £500 1st Prize and two £250 runners-up for the Best School in the country, a £20 cheque for the Best Poet, together with four £5 runners-up vouchers, for each county. Marketing is through the participating schools.

Ian Walton for **Triumph House** (Christian Poetry) says that the imprint is very new, but he as editor will choose what is to be included. Royalty levels will have to be assessed. Marketing will be through flyers to Christian newspapers and the local press. Unsolicited religious poetry accepted, with sae.

For **Fox Books**, Oak Tree, Main Road, Colden Common, Nr Winchester, Hants SO21 1TL tel: 0703 692309, Beryl Bron, Managing Editor, writes that she publishes 1 or 2 books a year, picked "by subjective opinion I'm afraid" she says. Royalties are paid where and after sales allow her to recoup costs – which rarely happens. Marketing is through the usual channels. "Poetry is not our main publishing output. I regard poetry as an accepted loss which is supported by our other publications," Beryl writes. Large and mighty book publishers *please nota bene*. Unsolicited manuscripts may be sent but only when accompanied by an sae – please!

Jeremy Page for **The Frogmore Press**, 42 Morehall Avenue, Folkestone, Kent CT19 4EK tel: 0303 275085, tells me that through their imprint **Crabflower Pamphlets** they publish 1 or 2 poets a year. The criteria for acceptance is on "quality alone." Royalties take the shape of 12 free copies and marketing is done through flyers, a 'titles in print' leaflet and through their *Frogmore Papers* magazine. Unsolicited manuscripts may be submitted with sae during January and February of each year.

John Black for **Frontier Publishing**, Windetts, Kirstead, Norfolk NR15 1BR tel: 0508 558174, tells me they are considering publishing poetry books but haven't as yet cracked the most pressing problem – how does one market a poet's book? "I believe," he says "poetry to be the oldest, most extensive, most sincere – and yet, most neglected literary form." No unsolicited manuscripts please.

G.

The **Gay Men's Press (GMP Publishers Ltd)**, P O Box 247, London N17 9QR tel: 081 365 1545 was founded some 10–15 years ago to publish books of interest to the gay community, though not necessarily written by gay authors. It had been found that the mainstream publisher was loath to publish books which included gay relationships or predominately gay issues. Managing Director Aubrey Walter tells me that they no longer publish poetry books, "because they didn't sell."

For **Ginn & Co Ltd**, Prebendal House, Parson's Fee, Aylesbury, Bucks HP20 2QZ tel: 0296 394442, Catherine Baker, Commissioning Editor, Reading, said they are bringing out *Poetry Express* in May of '94. A three poetry book reading series – the first book for 6–7 year olds, the second for 8–9 year olds, and the third for 10–12 – with all the poems for the series having been chosen by Sandy Brownjohn. Marketing is by direct mail, catalogue, educational reps visiting schools and other normal routes. Poems for children only.

THE ERIC GREGORY TRUST FUND AWARDS

Awards are made annually from this Fund for the encouragement of young poets.

The closing date for each year is October 31st of the *previous* year although it greatly assists the judges if entries can be sent in well before that date.

Candidates for the awards must:

1 Be British subjects *by birth* but not nationals of "Eire or any of the British Dominions or Colonies," and ordinarily resident in the United Kingdom or Northern Ireland.

2 Be under the age of 30 at 31st March in the year for which an entry is made.

3 Submit for consideration a published or unpublished volume of poetry, drama—poems (not more than 30), or belles—lettres.

The presentations are made annually in the summer of the year of the awards. Entries should be sent to The Society of Authors, 84 Drayton Gardens, London SW10 9SB, labelled on the envelope "Eric Gregory Trust Awards," with an accompanying letter from the candidate:

a Confirming that he is a British subject by birth.

b Giving his date of birth and normal place of residence.

c Enclosing an sae for the return of the poems.

The awards vary from year to year but as an example in 1993 there were six awards totalling £27,000.

Chairman and Editorial Head Dr S Y Killingley on behalf of **Grevatt & Grevatt,** 9 Rectory Drive, Newcastle Upon Tyne tel: 091 2858053, told me he would ideally like to publish one book or one anthology a year but funding makes it impossible. He chooses work that appeals to his own aesthetic senses and mainly publishes work from his academic colleagues. Royalties of 15% would be paid after the sale of the first 500 copies if that were to be achieved. Any profit made from books normally goes towards publishing minority interest works. Marketing is via reviews, *New Books* in the TLS, Whitakers and the British Library. Unsolicited work may be submitted but only five or six poems with an sae.

Jim Vollmar for the **Greylag Press,** 2 Grove Street, Higham Ferrers, Northants NN10 8HX tel: 0933 58373, writes that he would normally choose books to publish through his personal editorial taste, give a royalty of some 10–20 free copies and allow authors to buy copies at a 40% discount. Marketing the books was through mailings and reviews. At present however Greylag is in fact semi-dormant with no products planned other than a possible joint venture. He says that the question of marketing is the most relevant to the situation as he feels that, especially for the small press, it depends upon the author being active on its behalf. The other problem was in finding cheap but pleasing print quality. He is still willing to look at submissions but the chances of his taking any up are fairly remote.

H.

David Cobb on behalf of the **British Haiku Society,** 'Sinodun', Shalford, Nr Braintree, Essex CM7 5HN tel: 0371 851097, writes that they are unlikely to publish more than one book a year and that everything published will be commissioned. Marketing is through a newsletter to society members, pre–publication offers, launch parties, loan exhibitions, media articles, interviews and a distributor if the book warrants it. No unsolicited material is accepted.

Chairman and Managing Director John Hale for **Robert Hale Ltd** of 45–47 Clerkenwell House, Clerkenwell Green, London EC1R 0HT tel: 071 251 2661, feels they cannot "fairly be described as poetry publishers for they rarely publish more than one book a year, and then there are always special circumstances" and that they do not invite submissions.

For **Hamish Hamilton** – see Penguin

Kyra De Coninck for **Hangman Books**, 32 May Road, Rochester, Kent ME1 2HY tel: 0634 814477, tells me that they choose who to publish by what they feel to be suited to Hangman's high quality. Basically they have a flexible policy in that if they are really impressed by a poet they will either publish the poet under their own imprint at their own costs, or on a share–publishing basis, or they may advise the poet on how to go about self–publishing. They give a royalty of a third of wholesale price and market the books through review copies and press releases to relevant magazines. Unsolicited work may be submitted with a suitable sae.

On behalf of **Harvill Publishers**, 77–85 Fulham Palace Road, London W6 8JB tel: 081 741 7070, Bill Swainson writes that although they publish on average 2 or 3 books each year these are "in keeping with their translation paperback list which is mainly from European and other languages." They are the only imprint of **Harper Collins** to publish poetry regularly and have also published a couple of anthologies in the last 5 years. He feels though, that poets would be better served by submitting their work to regular poetry publishers rather than to Harvill.

For **Headland Publications,** 38 York Avenue, West Kirby, Wirral, Merseyside LA8 3JF tel: 051 625 9128, Gladys Mary Coles writes that they publish on average 8 poets a year. Consideration is on the "quality of poetry and the commitment of the poet" to his or her work. They pay 7% or the same value in copies as royalties and market their books through Password and other professional representation and distribution bodies.

Janice Whitten, the English Publisher for **Heinemann,** Halley Court, Jordan Hill, Oxford OX2 8EJ tel: 0865 311366, told me that "**Heinemann Educational** is a schools educational publisher rather than a poetry publisher. Therefore the poems we publish tend to be anthologies for 11–18 year olds. We usually publish poems which have not already been published elsewhere."

Roland John, founder of **Hippopotamus Press,** 22 Whitewell Road, Frome, Somerset BA11 4EL tel: 0373 466653, writes that they have published "at best six titles a year, at worst, two, though in 1994 we are to publish eight." He chooses those to be published through his "own critical decision" and he is looking "to publish verse by those writers who have learned from the Modernist Movement and have added their own distinct diction and metrical devices to those tenets. We are interested in work that is both imaginative and metrically distinguished." Their normal print run is 800 paperback and 200 cloth with the number of pages ranging between 50 and 300, though a preferred size is 64–96. Royalties are normally paid at 7½%. Marketing is through as much advertising as they can afford, reviews and occasionally Library Conference arrangements in the USA. Eighty per cent of sales are through bookshops and libraries with the balance by direct sale, book fairs and launches. They handle their own distribution in the UK and use State Mutual of New York in the USA. Virtually all their publications (with the exception of second or third books by the same author) occur through unsolicited submissions.

I.

Peter Dent for **Interim Press**, 3 Thornton Close, Budleigh Salterton, Devon EX9 6PJ tel: 0395 445231, says "Interim has been out of action for several years now," and that he is only "selling off old stock."

Peter Mortimer, Founding Editor of the **Iron Press**, 5 Marden Terrace, Cullercoats, North Shields, Tyne & Wear tel: 091 253 1901, writes that they average 2 books a year. These are usually poets who have been nurtured through *Iron Magazine*. Iron pay a straight £50 plus discontinued copies as a royalty and market their books through Password. Unsolicited submissions are not accepted for books.

J.

On behalf of **Jackson's Arm Press**, PO Box 74, Lincoln LN1 1QG (no telephone listing), Michael Blackburn tells me they publish 1 or 2 poets a year and specialise in promoting new poets. Royalties are in the form of 10% of the print run. Marketing includes prepublication offers, direct mail, swapped leaflets, bookshops and distribution through trade outlets. Unsolicited manuscripts will be considered (with sae) but most works are commissioned.

Managing Director Antony Jarrold for **Jarrold Publishing**,

Whitefriars, Norwich, Norfolk NR2 1JF tel: 0603 763300, writes that he doesn't feel they are really in the poetry publishing category though they have offered, as gift books, some poems designed to sell in large quantities (their *Shakespeare Collection* and *Poets Series* which includes Burns, Byron, Keats being examples). What they publish is usually as an extension of an existing range, "having a national appeal." They pay either a 5% royalty or outright fee where applicable and that although poets may submit unsolicited work, they will probably "receive it back with a polite letter."

For **Jonathan Cape** – see Cape

For **Michael Joseph** – see Michael

Cheryl Wilkinson, Director of **Jugglers Fingers Press**, 92 Staneway, Leam Lane, Gateshead, Tyne & Wear NE10 8LS tel: 091 2724491, says that they are hoping to publish individuals' collections from the end of this year (1994). Most of those published will stem from the magazine *Uncompromising Positions* which is funded by Sefton Arts development who it is hoped will also fund the books. Royalties will take the form of free copies. The books will be sold through a distributor, flyers and the usual publicity outlets. Unsolicited manuscripts welcome with sae.

K.

Senior Editor Caroline Walsh on behalf of **Kingfisher** (an imprint of **Larousse plc**), Elsley House, 24–30 Great Tichfield Street, London W1F 7AD tel: 071 631 0878, writes that they only publish anthologies of poetry for children by well-known poets. The editors (in the past Mike Rosen and Roger McGough) choose what to include. Various royalties are paid starting at 2½% for anthologists.

Marketing is through counterpacks, catalogues, review copies etc. Unsolicited work may be submitted with an sae but they do not publish volumes by single poets or for adults.

Kyle Cathie, Managing Director of **Kyle Cathie Ltd**, 7–8 Hatherley Street, London SW1P 2QT tel: 071 834 8027, says they only publish "popular out of copyright (in other words dead) poets." Marketing is to the general trade and specialist outlets throughout the world. Unsolicited submissions are most definitely discouraged.

L.
For **Larousse plc** – see Kingfisher

Publisher Rosemary Jones of **Littlewood Arc**, Nanholme Mill, Shaw Wood Road, Todmorden, Lancs OL14 6DA tel: 0706 812338, wrote that they publish between 8 and 10 books a year which are chosen by the editor – no anthologies. They pay 7½% royalties. Books are marketed through Password, reviews and advertising. Unsolicited work may be submitted with an sae but few books come from that source.

Joan Ward, Publisher of Poetry for **Longman Education**, Longman Group, Longman House, Burnt Mill, Harlow, Essex CM20 2JE tel: 0279 426721, told me that it would be easier if she were to send me their brochures.

In **The Longman Book Project**, which is for primary school children, there are 8 single–poem picture books by John Mole, Wes Magee and Judith Nicholls for infant--school children as well as a collection of rhymes and an anthology by Grace Hallworth.

For Junior school children, there are 5 collections by Brian Moses, David Orme, Fred Sedgwick and John

Cotton. There are narrative poems in picture-book format and an anthology of poems by women writers, also a Rap collection edited by Michael Rosen.

In **The Longman Literature** series for secondary pupils (Key Stage 3, Key Stage 4 and A level) they publish *Poems from Other Centuries* edited by Adrian Tissier and *Five Modern Poets* edited by Barbara Bleiman. Two further anthologies are in preparation as a part of the Longman Literature series for Spring 1995.

There is an extensive list of Shakespearean plays edited by Roy Blatchford with the series consultant Jackie Head and it is interesting to note that Longman carry an extensive **Modern Women Writers** series edited by Maura Healy which includes *A Quartet Of Poems* and *Fire The Sun*.

They have also published *The Poetry Of Protest* edited by Simon Fuller (a BBC-Longman joint venture), *Squeeze Words Hard* edited by Maureen Alcorn and Amanda Ebborn, and *The Poetry Of War* edited by Simon Fuller (another BBC-Longman joint venture). Apart from these there are also *Steps To Poetry* by Paul Groves, John Griffin and Nigel Grimshaw, and *Tradewinds* compiled and edited by R B Heath.

In their Key Stage 3 series they have Poetry Street 1, 2 and 3, compiled and edited by David Orme and James Sale.

Joan tells me that where there are only a few authors featured in an anthology she usually splits the royalties between them. Where there are many they each receive a straight fee. Marketing is by repping through schools and direct mail.

Rosalind Ward, Publisher for African and Caribbean Fiction, Caribbean Schoolbooks, **Longman International Education**, wrote that they publish poetry either within their *Writers Series* (African or Caribbean) for adult readership, or within a schoolbook format for children in

Africa or in the Caribbean. In both cases they publish anthologies rather than the collected works of one poet. In 1994 they are publishing *Sunsong Tide Rising*, an anthology for Caribbean schools. In 1995 they may include some poetry in an anthology of new writing from the Caribbean. Poets would be paid fees for inclusion of their work. Unsolicited poetry is rarely considered.

M.

Anthony Selbourne for **Making Waves**, PO Box 226, Guildford, Surrey GU3 1EW (no telephone listing), tells me that he publishes 2 or 3 poets annually, mostly from Nordic Countries (ie. translations) at present and in the immediate future. Choice of poet is through publisher contacts and specialist knowledge. Royalties depend upon individual contracts with writers, translators and publishing companies in other countries. Marketing is via the press, radio, magazine adverts, reviews, flyers and readings. Unsolicited material from UK writers is not encouraged except those already involved with the magazine *Making Waves*. Sae must always be enclosed as Anthony says "he does not subsidise postage."

Mandeville Press, 2 Taylor's Hill, Hitchen, Herts (no telephone listing), publish 4 books a year. Consideration is given by the dual editors, Peter Scupham and John Mole, to "excellence and formal quality." Royalties are free copies, extras plus a percentage. Marketing is by subscribers' list and reviews. Unsolicited work is not encouraged unless "by a genius!"

John Welch for **The Many Press**, 15 Norcott Road, London N16 7BJ tel: 081 806 5723, tells me that he publishes 2 to 3 poets a year, chosen by his own personal judgement. Payment is in free copies and marketing by mailing list and a few shops. Unsolicited manuscripts (with an sae) are welcome, though few new poets can be taken on.

Hamish Whyte for the **Mariscat Press**, 3 Mariscat Road, Glasgow G41 4ND tel: 041 423 7291, said they publish 1 poet a year. Choice is "subjective." Royalties are paid at 10%. Marketing is via flyers, reviews and repping. Unsolicited manuscripts may be submitted with an sae.

Barry Taylor for **Maypole Editions**, 65 Mayfair Avenue, Ilford, Essex 1GI 3DQ tel: 081 554 8670, writes that he publishes anthologies of, on average, six poets. He chooses "what he likes." Poets featured each receive 2 bound copies of the book. Marketing is through Teleordering, code MAYPOLE EDITIONS. Unsolicited manuscripts may be submitted with an sae.

For the **Menard Press**, 8 The Oaks, Woodside, London N12 8AR tel: 081 446 5571, Anthony Rudolf says they do not publish "Anglophone poets, only translations." His brochure contains translations from French, Russian, Portuguese, Serbo-Croat, Polish, German, Ugaritic (an extinct Semitic language from north Syria) and Walloon. When costs of translations have been met the translator receives a royalty which is separately negotiated for each book. Marketing in the UK or Ireland is through a distributor, Central Books (Troika), 99 Wallis Rd, London E9 5LN tel: 081 986 4854. Unsolicited work is considered "once in a while."

From the Editorial Department of **Michael Joseph** and **Pelham Books**, 27 Wright's Lane, London W8 5TZ tel: 071 416 3200, I am told that they published Spike Milligan's poetry because he was already an established author of theirs. They also publish works by other poets selected by David Owen – another of their authors – as well as *The Family Poetry Book*, a selection of poems chosen by celebrities and sold in aid of charity. They do not however wish to be sent unsolicited manuscripts.

N.

Helen Robinson, Editor and a Trustee of **The National Poetry Foundation 1981** (registered charity No 283032), 27 Mill Road, Fareham, Hants PO16 0TH tel: 0329 822218, says they publish between 11 and 25 books a year. Poetry accepted must say something of interest to a reader and show a poetic discipline or form. The NPF pays no royalties though the poet receives five free copies and may buy any additional copies required at £1 below selling price. Efforts are made to get the poet featured on radio and TV and in 'secular' magazines with any fees going directly to the poet. Marketing is through review, radio, some recital work and general publicity. The cost of producing the perfectly bound and laminated books is sponsored by Rosemary Arthur. No unsolicited work is considered, only that of NPF subscribers. The NPF gives grants, but *not* to poets to publish books of their own poetry.

Toni Savage for **New Broom Private Press**, 78 Cambridge Street, Leicester LE3 0JP tel: 0533 547419, says that he is a private printer and only produces 2 or 3 chapbooks a year, 100 or 200 copies of each. Also *Phoenix Sheets* (attractive single colour cards on which appears a poem and illustration) where both the poet and illustrator get free copies. Among many others, he has produced poems for Spike Milligan CBE in this genre.

O.

Ian Robinson for **Oasis Books**, 12 Stevenage Road, London SW6 6ES tel: 071 736 5059, writes that they publish on average 2 books a year but are hoping to increase this. He decides from the overall quality of the work whether to publish or not. They do not give royalties as such but give the author 25 copies of the book and a 40% or 50% discount on purchases. Marketing is by review copies, direct mail and a small catalogue. Poets are advised to examine previous publications before submitting.

For the **Only Women Press Ltd**, 71 Great Russell Street, London WC1B 3BN tel: 071 404 6227, the Managing Editor, Lilian Mohin writes to say they publish 3 or more books a year. A team of readers with both a Literary and Lesbian Feminist background suggest their choice. Royalties vary upwards from 10% of cover price. Marketing is to the book trade and through distributors.

Lilian stresses that they are a *Feminist* publisher and that they sponsor the UK's only award for Feminist poetry by Lesbian poets. Unsolicited manuscripts may be submitted with an sae.

Jacqueline Simms, Poetry Editor for **The Oxford University Press**, Walton Street, Oxford OX2 6DP tel: 0865 56767, says she publishes between 8 and 10 books a year, choosing what to publish by reading the manuscripts, pays the "normal paperback royalties" with a small advance, and that books are marketed through reviews, readings, poetry catalogues and adverts. Individuals may submit unsolicited work but only if it is a full collection (between 30–40 poems) and an sae *must* be enclosed.

P.

Ms Foufou Savitsky for the **Panrun Collective**, 8 Medora

Road, London SW2 2LN (telephone not listed), writes to tell me they publish one or two books a year. They publish the Creole language of the Caribbean, standard French and standard English. Choice is by general consent of the collective. There is a one off payment or a 20% royalty. Marketing is by mail order and performance. Unsolicited work is welcome with an sae.

Peter Stockill, Secretary of the **Paranoia Press**, 6 Brunner House, Langridge Crescent, Berwick Hills, Middlesborough, Cleveland TS3 7LF (no telephone listed), writes that they publish on average 4 books a year, which occasionally include other material apart from poetry (short stories, plays), however, they are mainly noted for poetry. They decide on who to publish on the grounds of "quality and locality" – they feel there should be a local theme or that the author should have a local connection. They used to pay 7–10% royalties, but now tend to provide complimentary copies instead. Marketing is through a book launch – often at *Writearound*, Cleveland's annual festival of writing and reading. The poets published also go on tour to regional and national venues. The books are reviewed in local magazines and featured at the Small Press book fair. Anyone may submit work with an sae, though they are advised to read a publication first.

Colin Stanley writing for **Pauper's Press**, 27 Melbourne Road, West Bridgford, Nottingham NG2 5DJ tel: 0602 815063, tells me that they do not publish books *of* poetry, but books *about poets* – mostly Literary critiques and essays about poets – such as Shamus Heaney, Peter Russell, Stanley Burnshaw, Peter Dale, Stevie Smith, Idris Davies and Francois Villon.

The contact for **Peepal Tree Books**, 17 Kings Avenue,

Leeds LS6 1QS tel: 0532 451703, is Jeremy Poynting. Peepal is "a radical third world publishing house with a particular focus on the Caribbean, South Asian diaspora, and the black British experience." They publish between 10 and 12 books a year of both new, established and neglected writers. Pay 10% royalties. Market their books through Password in the UK, Inland Books of America and Marginal in Canada.

For **Pelham Books** – see Michael Joseph

For **Penguin Group Children's Publishing**, 27 Wright's Lane, London W8 5TZ tel: 071 416 3000, Louise Jordan, Children's Reader, writes that they look for new, exciting material – poets who can competently use a strong, different voice. "I suppose it's the usual question of knowing it when we see it." They receive an average of 25 manuscripts a week. Royalties very much depend from person to person. Marketing includes performance by the poet in schools and to the public at large. Unsolicited manuscripts may be submitted.

Under the Penguin Group's imprint **Hamish Hamilton**, Editorial Director Jan Nissen tells me that they have only published 3 children's poetry titles in the last seven years and that any unsolicited manuscripts are passed on to **Viking/Blackie**'s Editorial Director Rosemary Stones, who tells me that they publish on average six hardbacks a year suitable for children age-range 6–16 and that they look for a poet who has a strong and very different 'voice'. They also receive around 25 poetry manuscripts a week. Marketing is done through standard routes, including performance by the poet in schools and to the general public. Unsolicited manuscripts should be marked for the attention of *Viking Blackie Children's Reader*. An sae is essential.

For Penguin's other imprints **Puffin** and **Fantail**, Editorial Director Philippa Milnes-Smith tells me she publishes on average 12 paperbacks a year. Royalties are variable and marketing through their standard routes. She says that they see several hundred manuscripts a year and choice is dependent on the quality of each. Unsolicited work should not be submitted to Puffin but to the hardback imprints above.

The publication plans of **Permanent Press**, 5B Compton Avenue, Canonbury, London N1 2XD tel: 071 359 6903 are in a state of "indefinite suspension," according to Robert Vas Dias.

Harry Chambers for the registered charity **Peterloo Poets**, 2 Kelly Gardens, Calstock, Cornwall PL18 9SA tel: 0822 833473, writes that he publishes 6-9 poets a year. That the criteria against which he decides who to publish is "solely that of quality - like A E Housman and Philip Larkin." He has no enthusiasm for too much cleverness or obscurity unless it is the kind that Philip Larkin called "luminous and wonder-generating." He is not keen on the poetic equivalent of abstract painting and prefers his poems to be peopled.

He finds that his *Peterloo Poets Open Poetry Competition* sometimes throws up a new poet in the prizewinners from whom he will invite a manuscript - this happened in the cases of Donald Atkinson and Maureen Wilkinson and is about to happen with Naomi Wallace (from the USA) and Anna Crowe, winner of the £2,000 first prize in the 1993 competition.

Peterloo Poets have a standard contract which is drawn up before publication and which largely follows the Society of Authors' suggestions. There is a £50 advance paid to the poet in the case of a first volume and £100 in the case of subsequent ones, against royalties of 10%.

THE ROYAL SOCIETY OF LITERATURE AWARD
Under the W H Heinemann bequest

Publishers are invited to submit books for the above award. Books submitted must have been published during the current year and must be written in the English Language; translations are not eligible for consideration.

The purpose of the bequest is the encouragement of genuine contributions to literature. The Testator, however, wished the Committee to give preference to those publications which are less likely to command big sales – eg poetry, biography, criticism, philosophy, history – though novels, if of sufficient distinction, will not be overlooked.

The Committee would be especially interested in the work of younger authors who are not yet widely recognised, but the work of well–known authors will not thereby be excluded from consideration.

One, two or three prizes may be given, though the Committee reserves the right to withhold an award if no work, in their opinion, is considered to be of sufficient merit.

Publishers should forward one copy of each book to the Secretary, labelling it "W H Heinemann Prize." The closing date for entries is October 31st.

Recent prize winners have been:

> 1992 John Gross   *Shylock*
> 1991 Nicholas Boyle *Göethe: the Poet and the Age*
> 1990 Roy Fuller   *Available for Dreams*
> and Kit Wright   *Short Afternoons*

The Royal Society of Literature, 1 Hyde Park Gardens, London W2 2LT tel: 071 723 5104.

Marketing is through 3,000 full colour fliers sent to his private mailing list, library suppliers and bookshops; launch readings; volumes repped to the booktrade by Password. Peterloo also print an annual catalogue/stocklist and have an Associate Membership scheme which offers members discounted books. Unsolicited manuscripts must be accompanied by a suitable and large enough sae – not just *loose stamps* without a return envelope – and the manuscript should not be ring bound or have "silly plastic grippers."

Margaret E. Rose, the General Editor of **Pickpockets**, 25 St Mary's Terrace, Hastings, East Sussex TN34 3LS tel: 0424 714393, writes that they publish 3 or 4 poets a year and of the living poets, "we give preference to local writers. We do not pay royalties, but a lump sum which varies according to status." Marketing is direct to bookshops, museums, theatres and a current list is sent to individuals. Margaret sent me five very attractively illustrated (black ink line drawing) A6, twelve and fourteen page individual booklets of poetry. They do not encourage unsolicited submissions.

Peter Riley of **Poetical Histories**, 27 Sturton Street, Cambridge CB1 2QG tel: 0223 327455, publishes small works of about 6 poets annually. Chooses what he sees as "contributing to a sense of the nature and purpose of poetry that I wish to further." No charges, no royalties. Marketing mainly by subscription but also through normal book–selling channels. Prefers to seek out poets himself, rather than from unsolicited manuscripts.

Peter Sansom and Janet Fisher are together, directors of **The Poetry Business Ltd**, 51 Byram Arcade, Huddersfield HD1 1ND tel: 0484 434840. Peter tells me that their imprint **Smith/Doorstop Books** publishes at most 5 or 6 perfect bound books and 8 pamphlets a year. He and Janet choose what to publish on the criteria of "excellence of work. We pay 45% discount on royalty exclusive copies and 10% royalties." They market through their own catalogue and Password. Few of their books are from unsolicited manuscripts.

For **Poetry Now Publications** – see Forward Press

For **Poetry Now Young Writers** – see Forward Press

For **Polygon,** 22 George Square, Edinburgh, Scotland EH8 9LF tel: 031 650 4689, Editorial Director Marion Sinclair told me they have 26 titles on their shelves at present and publish 2 books a year. Robert Crawford, Editor of *Verse,* and Polygon's Poetry Editor, chooses poets from manuscripts submitted and looks for new talent through his own magazine. They pay "normal royalties" and a £200 advance. Marketing is through poetry leaflets and other usual outlets. Unsolicited work may be submitted with sae.

Peter Geoffrey Paul Thompson (one person!) of the **Precious Pearl Press,** 71 Harrow Crescent, Romford, Essex RM3 7BJ tel 0708 370963, says they have published 1 poet so far and are hoping to publish 1 or 2 a year. The poetry is picked on "quality" and the poet receives 60% of the profit from his book. Marketing is via review copies.

P E Larkin for **Prest Roots Press,** 34 Alpine Court, Kenilworth, Warwickshire CV8 2GP tel: 0926 59278, writes that they publish 2 or 3 books a year. Decide who to publish by "foreknowledge." Do not pay royalties. Market their books through bookshops, catalogues, book

THE SIGNAL POETRY AWARD

The Signal Poetry Award
highlights excellence in
poetry published for children.
The most important aspect of the award
is the writing it prompts,
the award selectors being given as much space
as they need in each May issue of SIGNAL
to discuss their views on the winner
and on other poetry books
published during the year.
The award carries a prize of £100
and is marked by a certificate designed by
Michael Harvey, the eminent letterform designer.

All poetry books for children published in
Britain are eligible regardless of their
original country of publication.
Unpublished work is not eligible.

SIGNAL is the thrice–yearly specialist
journal devoted to the many aspects of
children's books:
critical, educational, historical, personal.

Thimble Press, Lockwood, Station Road,
Woodchester, Stroud, Gloucester GL5 5EQ.

* * *

Staple FIRST EDITIONS

Publication of writers in collection form: a biennial award which alternates with Staple Open Poetry Competition. SAE to Staple for details of project currently operating.

FIRST EDITIONS

1 Open to writers of poetry or prose.

2 Publication offered in a series with a growing reputation. First edition monograph award: 'Staple are to be congratulated on giving Jennifer Olds her first UK publication'; 'if competitions conjure up such work then they are indeed worthwhile.' *PN Review, Envoi.*

3 Handsome format – FIRST EDITION showcase award: 'Quintet is a well-produced book containing a selection of poems by five talented writers.' *Ore.*

4 Guaranteed circulation: publications to date have each sold 600 copies.

5 10% royalty, cash advance, complimentary and (optional) discount copies.

6 Copyright retained by authors.

7 No financial or purchase commitment required beyond initial reading fee (£10), which is refunded to all writers published in the series.

Please Note: Typescripts must satisfy the published conditions and can be accepted only during the periods designated for submission, though Staple itself is an always-open magazine of New Writing.

Staple FIRST EDITIONS, Tor Cottage, 81 Cavendish Road, Matlock DE4 3HD.

SUNDAY TIMES

SMALL PUBLISHER COMPETITION

A prize of £1,000 presented annually to an independent British publisher producing between 5 and 40 titles a year.

The final entry date is in February and the winner is announced in March. There are three judges: two from the Sunday Times and one from the Independent Publishers Guild, who administer the competition.

This award was set up to mark the launch of the *Sunday Times Books Supplement* in 1988. Previous winners are Fourth Estate, Serpent's Tail, Bloodaxe and Cornerhouse (shared), Verso, Blackstaff Press, Polygon, and Nick Hern Books.

Further details from

Independent Publishers Guild (STSP)
25 Cambridge Road
Hampton
Middlesex
TW12 2JL
tel: 081 979 0250

fairs and readings. Unsolicited submissions are not accepted.

For **Puffin** – see **Penguin**.

R.

Dermot Bolger for **Raven Arts**, P O Box 1430, Finglas, Dublin 11, Republic of Ireland, tells me that sadly, it closed down in 1992. It used to publish between 10 and 15 books a year which were chosen by an editorial board, paid 10% royalties and marketed the books through interviews and readings.

For **Red Candle Press**, 9 Milner Road, Wisbech, Cambridgeshire PE13 2LR tel: 0945 581067, Helen Gordon tells me they publish a few pamphlets, give a £10 advance on them and send an information leaflet to booksellers. The RCP specialises in "traditional poetry." Unsolicited manuscripts (with sae) welcome.

Christopher Mills for the **Red Sharks Press**, 122 Clive Street, Grangetown, Cardiff CF1 7JE tel: 0222 231696, writes that they publish between 5 and 7 books a year. Choice depends on "availability of funds and quality of writing." Royalties are in the form of 50% of profits. Marketing by reviews, leaflets, catalogue and readings. Unsolicited material *most definitely* **not** accepted.

From **Rockingham Press**, 11 Musley Lane, Ware, Herts SG12 7EN tel: 0920 467868, David Perman says he publishes some 6 books a year and choice is simply on "whether I like their poems." Royalties are 10% (5% in advance) plus 10 free copies. Marketing is through repping to bookshops and the poets being encouraged to sell books at readings. Unsolicited manuscripts may be submitted but it may take "up to 9 months for me to answer."

S.

Mark Robinson, the editor of **Scratch**, 9 Chestnut Road, Eaglescliffe, Stockton-on-Tees TS16 0BA tel: 0642 788835, tells me that he expects to publish on average 3 poets a year who invariably come through submissions to *Scratch Magazine*. Royalties take the shape of 50 free copies of the book and the poet being able to buy further copies at half price. Mark markets the books by reviews, leaflets, exposure with his magazine, and would advise anyone wishing to be considered for a book to submit work (with sae) for the magazine first.

For **Skoob Books Publishing Ltd** and its imprints **Skoob Pacifica** and **Skoob esoterica,** Editorial Office, 43 Old Bethnal Green Road, London E2 6PR (no telephone listing), Christopher Johnson, Editorial Director, tells me that they publish on average one or two UK poets and fewer than five from the Pacific Rim, each year. They hope to increase the number published but that is rather dependent on the expansion of their USA distribution system. Most of the publications are in English with the exception of Malay. Royalties are 7½% of net receipts and marketing through adverts in poetry magazines, reviews, poetry readings, distribution reps and through their *Skoob Books/Index On Censorship* International bi-annual poetry competitions.

For **Smith/Doorstop Books** – see Poetry Business Ltd

Allen Fisher on behalf of **Spanner**, 14 Hopton Road, Hereford HR1 1BE tel: 0432 277857, says he publishes 3 books a year. He himself decides who to publish. The poet pays for the publication of his own book but then receives at least 10 free copies. Marketing is done through distributors and ALP. Unsolicited manuscripts welcome but must be accompanied by an sae. Poets should read Spanner examples before submitting work - much of what is published would be thought of as experimental or innovative.

Paul Green for **Spectacular Diseases**, 83B London Road, Peterborough Cambs PE2 9BS (no telephone number available), told me they publish on average 3 books a year by invitation. They pay no royalties, market through "normal publicity" and only accept "experimental poetry." Poets are advised to write and enquire (with sae) before submitting work.

Donald Measham who co-edits **Staple First Editions**, Tor Cottage, 81 Cavendish Road, Matlock, Derbyshire DE4 3HD tel: 0629 582764, with Bob Windsor, says they publish 7 books over a two year period which they are hoping to increase to 4 a year. There is a panel of four which decides their editorial policy - "decidedly we do not publish our mates," he writes. There is a £5 reading fee per volume which is returnable if publication is taken up. Royalties take the form of an advance of £75 and 6 complimentary copies, with an option to purchase further copies at the normal price. Marketing is through a supplement in their own magazine *Staple* and through a selection of bookshops.

T.

Kenny Mackenzie, The Editor of **Taranis Books**, 2 Hugh Miller Place, Edinburgh EH3 5JG (no telephone listing), reports that they publish on average 5 books a year. He makes the decision as to what to publish and the work accepted is "fairly modern." Their basic royalty is 10% of sales, although this is often paid in copies at trade price. Marketing is by launch, limited advertising, mail shots and promotion at literary events and book festivals. A poet should submit a *small* sample of work with sae and await the invitation to submit further poems.

For **Triumph House** (Christian Poetry) – see Forward

Peter Ellson for **Tuba Press**, Route des Vans, La Republique, 30160 Bordezac, Gard, France tel: 010 33 66 25 02 98, writes to tell me that he publishes 4 English language poetry books a year. Chooses what to publish by "quality of work" submitted. Gives 10% of the trade price as royalties. Markets his books through readings, Foyles, the usual listings and reputation of his imprint. Unsolicited manuscripts welcome with international reply coupons (remember their individual value and send sufficient).

U.

For the last decade James Hogg has been editor of **The University Of Salzburg Press**, (Department of English and American Studies), Akademiestr. 24, A–5020 Salzburg, Austria tel: 010 43 662 80440. He publishes between 4 and 12 British poets annually and these are chosen from those he knows personally, or from those who have been recommended to him. The books range in size from some 200 pages to a massive 615 (*Trawling Tradition* by Desmond O'Grady).

He doesn't pay royalties but poets are given between 10 and 50 free copies and may purchase additional copies at cost. Marketing is done through many of the best known poetry magazine editors in this country. I am told that although James is to retire in 1996, there is every chance he will continue with his invaluable work.

V.

Richard Price, Co–editor/Manager of **Vennel Press**, 9 Pankhurst Court, Caradon Close, London E11 4TB (ex-

WHITBREAD BOOK OF THE YEAR

These annual awards for a Novel, First Novel, Children's Novel, **Poetry** and Biography are administered by three organisations, Whitbread; Whitbread's sponsorship consultancy, Kallaway Ltd; and the Booksellers Association of Great Britain.

The Booksellers Association is responsible for administration including the collection of books from publishers and their distribution to the judges and subsequently the promotion of the winners to booksellers. Kallaway Ltd liaises with BA to invite appropriate judges and oversee the judging process and stage–manages the annual Book of the Year Dinner at the Brewery in the City.

Whitbread are anxious to recognise writers who live and work in the UK or Ireland, irrespective of nationality, thus to be eligible a writer must be domiciled in the UK or Eire for the previous three years and be published between 1st November of the previous year and 31st October of the year of submission of the entry.

Entries are invited in June each year when the category judges are also announced. Mid/end of July sees the deadline for entries. October heralds the shortlist in each category. Early November the category winners are announced followed in December by the announcement of the final judging panel. The Whitbread Book of the Year Dinner is held in late January.

For full details contact the Secretary, Lorna Peppiatt, The Booksellers Association, Minster House, 172 Vauxhall Bridge Road, London SW1V 1BA tel: 071 834 5477.

directory), writes that they publish one or two poets a year. A collection of work emerges through the network of poets with whom Vennel is associated. Royalties are subject to negotiation. Marketing is through adverts, a mail list, Whitakers and book fairs. Unsolicited manuscripts (with sae) will be considered.

For **Viking** – see **Penguin**

Melanie Silgardo on behalf of **Virago**, The Rotunda, 42–43 Gloucester Crescent, Camden Town, London NW1 7PD tel: 071 916 6066, writes to tell me that they publish two individuals' volumes of poetry a year but that as the space for individual poets is so limited the decision as to whom to publish is a hard one. "We tend to publish poets whose work we represent anyway e.g. Maya Angelou, Margaret Atwood, Grace Paley, Grace Nichols, etc. They tend to be fairly well established in the main, but not always. For example, next year (1995) we will be publishing the work of Janice Mirikitani, a Japanese American poet whose work is not known in Britain at all but whose territory is a vastly unexplored one."

"In 1993 we launched *Virago New Poets*, an anthology of poets who had not yet published solo volumes. We spread the net widely for this and did not solicit work from particular poets, but depended solely on work that was sent in in response to our nationwide call. We hope that *Virago New Poets* will become a regular biennial platform for new unpublished poets. We also publish at least one thematic anthology every year and we've had some tremendous success with *The Virago Book Of Love Poetry* and *The Virago Book Of Wicked Verse*."

"In answer to your question, we're not specifically a 'women's poetry publisher' we are a women's publishing house, and the need for there to be one has not diminished.

With the exception of a couple of poetry publishers, I think new women poets do feel, on the whole (in an area where it's difficult enough to publish anyway) that it's still tough to break into the old network. This will all change in time I'm sure, but it hasn't yet. I don't think there's a conspiracy, just a very blind spot. Those more enlightened construct a fifty–fifty structure so everyone's happy – at least there's an awareness of an imbalance that needs to be corrected."

Virago pays an advance against royalties of 7½%. Marketing is through flyers and leaflets targeted at an extensive mailing list. They organise readings and radio interviews where possible. They send out word–of–mouth copies to writers and poets who may be in a position to talk about the book and review copies are sent to editors and columnists nationwide. They, to use Melanie's own words, "Unfortunately tend to discourage unsolicited manuscripts because of the size of our poetry list."

W.

John Catley for the **Wellsweep Press**, 1 Grove End House, 150 Highgate Road, London NW5 1PD tel: 071 267 3525, tells me that they publish on average 2 books a year. Choice depends on availability of material in good translation (they only publish from the Chinese). There is normally a flat fee. Marketing is done through the UK and US distributers, trade channels and readings. Unsolicited work is not recommended unless the writer is involved with Chinese Literature.

Bob Cobbing for **Writers Forum**, 89a Petherton Road, London N5 2QT tel: 071 226 2657, writes that they publish on average 18 books but only "experimental poetry – concrete, shaped, visual, sound, performance, etc and publish what surprises and excites us." The poet receives 12 copies of his book free and sometimes a fee of

£60 and travelling expenses for a launch. Marketing is usually at events, mail-order and publicity through ALP Newsletter and Catalogue and PALPI. Unsolicited submissions are accepted, but the poet should find out the sort of work published before submitting his own.

* * *

These then were publishers listed in the recognised and respected reference manuals as publishers of poetry. But what of those advertising widely in the national newspapers and national magazines, yet not found in the these reference books? It is, after all, to these reference books that people turn when looking for a publisher, so why were't they? In them, I mean.

The answers to the question "what is vanity press" have always been about as useful as the answers to the question "what is poetry." Sometimes too glib, sometimes well thought out, sometimes biased, but invariably unsatisfactory and incomplete.

Vanity press was airily dismissed as 'anyone who pays another to publish his work' – normally a reflection on the ability of, and intended as an insult to, the poet not the publisher – clearly a nonsense, for as we have already seen many poets in the past were forced to pay to get to their public initially and in today's climate, of far too many poets chasing far too few genuine publishers and far too little sponsorship, it has become the accepted norm that some may have to contribute to the cost of their publication. And what *if* . . . Grandad decides he wants to leave a small book of his poems to his family and pays to have the book published. Is this vanity press or simply a perfectly understandable wish that has little 'vain' about it? Perhaps it is Grandad's grandchildren who have cajoled him into the enterprise and, that being the case (and if it *is* vanity to

48

publish in those circumstances), whose vanity is it – his or theirs?

In the past if we wished to belittle someone's book we only needed to call it a vanity publication for everyone else to nod sagely and dismiss the offending tome as somehow seedy and less than 'nice' – the poetry it contained somehow demeaned in quality due to the Judas shillings spent – when really vanity publishing has more to do with who publishes, and under what terms, than with who is published.

We are often decrying the innocent and unaware for being so, while letting the black marketeer creep by unaccountable, if we continually accuse poets of 'vanity publishing' when what we *should* be asking is, "in what way is the poet being disadvantaged by a company advertising a publication service which may be found less than genuine?" And, "in what way is 'less than genuine', less than genuine?" Is it perhaps simply a question of lack of experience in the publication of poetry where the publisher is concerned, rather than anything nasty or underhand? Just the blind leading the blind? Or is there under the label 'vanity press' a bevy of heartless publishing houses hell–bent on fleecing anyone innocent enough to believe their 'come–on'?

The majority of those who approach advertisers in the national press are not the established poets, but the inexperienced, the innocent and the amateur, with little or no idea of what to expect from a publisher; what *is* genuine and knowledgeable comment; what promises of marketing *are* real, attainable, and *can* be supported; what *is* a fair price for their book.

Poets with such a slight understanding of the market place can only be excused when, having written to a company which tells them (for instance) that their work is "well crafted and worthy of publication", they believe it. You'd think national newspapers and magazines would

49

have vetted any advert appearing in their pages. The amount of money these adverts cost you'd think there'd be enough to organise a vetting service on behalf of those who are to answer them? Those who directly make advertisers advertise in the first place. Leave that one for the Newspaper mogul!

A company giving an honest editorial appraisal of the work submitted or admitting that they are not qualified to do so; advertising a fair charge for publishing the book and at the same time advising the poet that the chances of him getting his outlay back from sales is nigh impossible (unless, perhaps, he is well known in some other field) as the only people likely to buy the book are his own friends and family – *would* be giving a good service. But does that actually happen? How often does it happen?

No–one is going to pass out the most encouraging editorial report on work submitted while at the same time promising to market the book and give the poet royalties that are higher than all other publishers – large enough sales to return the initial outlay – and in the same breath announce that what they do is in the interests solely of their own back pocket and that the poet is unlikely to see much of his outlay return. Such an outlet would soon be out of business.

There is an element to advertising that offers to publish your book for a charge or on a share–publishing basis which needs to be understood . . . whereas a publisher might give a worthwhile service to those writing prose (the market for a novel, thriller or romance being larger and more open) the same company would find it impossible to give a similar back–up service to a poetry book even with an extensive knowledge of both poetry and the market. But either wilfully, or from a lack of understanding of poetry, or from a lack of knowledge of the market, some advertisers seem to offer the self–same service to the poet as they do to the writer of prose.

So how to test the water? How find out just what the situation really is for the aspiring poet looking for a genuine and knowledgeable publisher?

Though there are many bona fide publishers who do advertise in the national press, it has also been argued that it is only the vanity press who can afford to do so. But to write to all openly asking each if it is genuine would be a complete waste of time and paper. The most blatant vanity publisher would claim industrious and philanthropic effort on behalf of all its clients – protest that it is each of the others who are vanity, *never* it itself! One would be none the wiser.

But it is amongst those who advertise (I was assured) I would find the real McCoy. The *real* vanity publisher – but how to set about it? Then I remembered that back in the early '70s I had cobbled together three unspeakably disastrous poems and sent them to Atlantic Press and Willow Press (both of whom have, I believe, long since ceased to trade). Each, during November of '72 wrote back expressing a wish to publish the poems (if I paid a huge fee for each one) with comments such as "style and metre good . . . story line graphic . . . I have little hesitation in representing this work as suitable for publication." Atlantic Press even sent me a Certificate of Special Mention which I still have.

Here then was the way. Set up a 'quality control' situation to test each and every one fairly and in an identical manner. Without, as one would say, any malice aforethought, or preconceived idea as to the validity, genuineness or otherwise, of any one of those to whom the 'quality control' poems were to be sent.

CHAPTER II

During the period October to December 1993 I scoured the national newspapers and magazines for advertisements offering to publish or help to publish a book, whether they mentioned poetry or not. The list consisted of Excalibur Press, Minerva Press, Adelphi Press, A H Stockwell, Avon Books, Dorrance Publishing, The Book Guild, Quest Publishing Co, Regency Press, The Pentland Press, The Short Run Print Co, Godfrey, and Janus Publishing. It was amongst these, if anywhere, the 'vanity press' were to be found.

Under the pseudonym of Roberts and an accommodation address I sent three poems I had concocted to each of the above. Where there appeared to be two companies trading as one, or one company with two names trading from different addresses . . . Adelphi and Excalibur advertising from different addresses but with the same telephone number, and Pentland Press at 1 Hutton Close, Bishops Aukland, with Editorial Office (W) at 5 Hutton Close, Bishops Aukland . . . I used the pseudonym of Locke and a further accommodation address and sent the same poems to both addresses.

John Burke of **Avon Books,** Dovedale Studios, 465 Battersea Park Road, London SW11 4LR tel: 071 924 2979, sent me a 'submission form' together with a standard introductory letter and a three page publishing prospectus in which he offered to submit my manuscript to an outside editor, who would give "a frank assessment of its potential" for publication. There was a mini potted history of the trials of getting published as an unknown, details of how to lay out work for submission (which I ignored), a promise to pay royalties and to send the author six complimentary copies followed by the statement that the more copies of your book that they sold "the more profit both you and we make." Finally he stressed the importance of getting reviews "local to the author and in national daily and Sunday newspapers."

I rang John Cox of **Axxent Ltd (The Short Run Print Co)**, 99–101 St. Leonard's Road, Windsor, Berks SL4 3BZ tel: 0753 857349 and he assured me that he doesn't publish poetry at all, publishing only prose books from supplied computer discs.

Lisa Kirkpatrick, UK Co–ordinator of **Dorrance Publishing Co Inc**, 50 New Bond Street, London W1Y 9HA tel: 071 495 3596, sent me a 32 page magazine containing details of books they'd published, details of how to select a subsidy publisher and pointing out that "[subsidy press] catalogues are sprinkled with names of authors who went on to bigger and better things," giving an example of one who had won a National Book Award and subsequently a National Book Critics' Circle Award having first had a book of poems published by Dorrance. This with the invitation, "from our initial review we would now be most interested to review more of your poetry."

Peter Nicholas, Director of **Arthur H. Stockwell Ltd**, Elms Court, Torrs Park, Ilfracombe, Devon EX34 8BA tel: 0271 862557, sent me a pamphlet of their latest publications, together with a letter thanking 'Roberts' for the three poems entitled Cenotaph, Love and Evening, "which we have received with interest," going on to explain the need for a payment from 'Roberts' if they were to publish the book but that they would make no charge for reading the ms and that they "looked forward to the pleasure of reading your additional manuscript . . ."

J Lyons of **Excalibur Press of London**, 138 Brompton

Road, London tel: 071 371 9044, sent a glossy booklet entitled *Help* and a Literary Panel editor's report signed by Ed Beerbohm which said "This author's work is of a good standard and shows potential," going on to ask for further work so that an assessment could be made.

J Lyons of **The Adelphi Press**, 4–6 Effie Road, London tel: 071 371 9044, sent 'Locke' a glossy booklet entitled *Help* together with a letter explaining "what are today, really, the only two avenues left for the publications of the new or little known authors and poets; self–publishing and subsidy publishing."

It will be noted that the text in both these *Help* booklets appear to be identical (pictures different), except in Excalibur's (on the bottom of page 15) they pay 40% royalties, whereas in Adelphi's (on the bottom of page 15) only 30% is paid. Both booklets are copyright 1967 J. West – the one (Excalibur) being a revised edition of the other.

The booklet starts by explaining what happens when you submit a manuscript to an average publisher – backed up by the experience of various famous books – and goes on to explain subsidy publishing with an eventual list of "Questions authors most often ask and the answers."

Anthony Phillips, Editorial Director of **The Pentland Press Ltd**, 1 Hutton Close, South Church, Bishop Auckland, Durham DL14 6XB tel: 0388 776555, sent both 'Locke' and 'Roberts' a glossy magazine of books published together with a standard letter stating that the three poems were "certainly thought provoking pieces," and going on to explain how the poet would be expected to invest at least £3,500 with an average being in the region of £5,500 – this investment should then be recouped from the revenue from the sales of the book. A royalty (he states) of 15% which "is considerably in excess of conventional publishers' rates" is paid. 'Locke' and 'Roberts' had each applied, one to Pentland at 1 Hutton Close, the other to '(Editorial Office W)' at 5 Hutton Close. Different publishers?

Carol Biss, Editorial Director of **The Book Guild Ltd**, Temple House, 25 High Street, Lewes, East Sussex BN7 2LU tel: 0273 472534, sent me a large wodge of cuttings from such as The Daily Telegraph, The Sun, The Daily Mail, The Evening Sentinel, The Times (to name but a few) reviewing (mainly) novels and autobiographies published by the Book Guild. A glossy 'Autumn/Winter Selection' arrived, together with a letter stating that "contributing to your book is not to be thought of as an investment . . . publishing is a risky business . . . we do hope this doesn't sound too negative . . . it is quite possible to lose money . . . you will appreciate it will take time to evaluate the text."

John Thorpe, Manager of **Regency Press (London and New York) Ltd**, 125 High Holborn, London WC1V 6QA tel: 071 242 8481, sent a compliments slip, scribbled upon which was a note to the effect that "we only produce private editions, details herewith," and enclosed a standard small pamphlet which starts off, "we have come to the conclusion that a small book of poems would not sell except through local bookshops and to friends of the author."

Terrance Godfrey of **Godfrey**, Nut Lane, Old Leake, Boston, Lincs PE22 9JF tel: 0205 871439, said he didn't publish poetry books at all.

David Hall (Publication Director) of **Minerva Press**[1], 2 Old Brompton Road, London SW7 3DQ tel: 071 225

[1] NB*This 'Minerva' must in no way be confused with Minerva, Michelin House, 81 Fulham Road, London SW3 6RB tel: 071 581 9393, a part of the* **Reed International Books Group.**

3113, sent 'Roberts' a two page letter in which he outlines "how our partnership plan works" which is "the only way that new authors can realistically expect to achieve publication and distribution of their work," going on to say that "the author is required to make a financial contribution towards the origination costs, but is pleasantly rewarded by the high level of royalties that we pay, which are very much higher than those of most publishers . . . of course, your book must be of a sufficiently high standard to merit publication by Minerva Press."

Janus Publishing Company, Duke House, 37 Duke Street, London W1M 5DF tel: 071 486 8591, did not reply – I subsequently discovered (when I rang them) that I had put the wrong road on my accommodation address and the answer (to 'Miss Locke') had gone astray.

"Silly girl, not even knowing her own address," I quipped to Janus, and 'she' was forgiven for being a 'silly girl'. Details would be sent – a second time!

Quest Publishing Co, 108 New Bond Street, London W1Y 9AA had disappeared from the face of the earth when someone went to enquire on my behalf after my initial letter wasn't answered and no telephone number could be found for them.

So, there were the immediate reactions to my three poems. Generally very helpful. A lot of information given and (hardly surprising), most of the companies giving the impression that they were the best, the most experienced and highest royalty–paying and therefore the only one to whom I should be safely entrusting my manuscript.

Nothing wrong with that and no more or less than one would expect. Certainly they are all right when they claim that some now established and respected authors had to pay to get their first book published. But it should be noted that in nearly every case these were not *poets* for whom *these publishers* had published books of poetry, who had subsequently become mildly or gigantically famous, but the novelist, the thriller writer, or the romancier who had printed   privately.

All that aside, if I had submitted my work to only one publisher, from the information I had been supplied I would certainly have been encouraged to go on and send my full manuscript and even after having submitted to all I could find, it would be no more than a question of personal preference in deciding to whom I would entrust the task of publishing my poems.

But what of the three poems I had contrived? Before you are able to judge the validity of these replies, and those to come in the subsequent pages, you need to read what was submitted. The poems appear on the following page.

Evening

The seagull flies o'er my head,
And the blue sea rushes with white horses,
By the beach to greet me,
And I feel free.
Because the sun is going down –
Feel like I am wearing a crown of gold –
Like a halo burnished of,
The setting sunshine.

Love

I held you in my arms at Christmas.
You must have thought me very brash!
The holly and the tinsel spoke to us,
of love and all the presents too.
I gave you socks of blue;
you gave me undies of a different hue.
And when we sang the carols me
and you (such pretty songs)
I blushed to think of
later ons.

Cenotaph

It is the old people who want to keep war alive,
They think it is a proud way to survive,
By praising it in lots of different ways.

They know that God will keep them safe
and look after the crying waifs.
We know you should not praise any war,

the Gulf, the Korean or the Boer,
If you want there not to be
any war – not any more!

CHAPTER III

Having received a first reaction from the advertisers, the next stage was to submit a full-blown ms to each. But where to get one? It was asking too much of dedication to actually sit down and write some 40 poems specifically for this exercise!

Fortunately we'd just come to the end of sifting for the shortlisted six entries for the Rosemary Arthur Award 1994 and among those that had not been shortlisted was a collection which I felt fitted the bill exactly. So I wrote to the author and received his written permission to submit them *under my own pseudonym to any advertisers I had previously chosen.*

It had been suggested to me by some who had submitted work to various outlets in the past that there was a possibility "no-one actually read the poems." Totally unfounded I was sure. But to prove a point, where a company asked for 64 poems I submitted our 40 together with photocopies of 25 of the original 40 mixed in. Elsewhere, 40 poems with 8 copies of copies – if you see what I mean? In fact to play fair, I sent a minimum of 48 copies of the 40 poems to everyone to see if the duplications would be noticed – as I was sure they would be.

Here again I feel it necessary to print the poems that I submitted so that you, the reader, know with what the publishers were dealing, and the work upon which they had been invited to comment with a view to publication.

In this chapter you will find a complete reproduction of all the poems I submitted, except that the typos have been corrected . . .

Sunday Morning

Sunday morning lazy feeling
Watch the dawning on the ceiling.
Early light comes ever creeping
Giving sight to end our sleeping.
Birds start singing, break of day.
Helios is chasing the darkness away.

Games I've Played

I've played many games across the years,
Cards and darts, dominoes and pool.
But looking back, through lonely tears,
The one I played best was the fool.

So many times I turned and fled,
From the aching of a broken heart,
Or, mayhap, from the thoughts in my head,
When they were tearing my very soul apart.

The search for knowledge was my quest,
Yet I ne'er saw the love offered to me.
An overactive mind that knows no rest,
And struggles, vainly, to be free.

Alas, now comes the Autumn of my life,
And I look back to count the cost.
A lonely man, no girlfriend or wife,
So the most important game I've lost.

Freedom

My mind roams freely, like a cloud,
Floating o'er trees and hills and dale.
Liberated from its mortal shroud,
Confined no longer to that material jail.

Lingering 'pon high, riding the breeze,
Drifting where the gentle winds blow,
Wandering, carefree, where e'er I please,
Concerned not o'er the direction I go.

And thus I tour where e'er I may,
With the ease of thought it would seem.
Then, alas, comes the break of day,
And I am awakened from my dream.

Springtime Rain

Watch the warm springtime rain,
Streaking across the windowpane.
Falling gentle to the ground,
Replenishing plants that abound.

See them grow so green and strong,
Amazing blooms will form e'er long.
Colours so rich for all to see,
Delicate petals of such beauty.

Raindrops trickle down tranquil leaf,
Hang, suspended, in stark relief.
Globule pure 'gainst live canopy,
An instant captured for eternity.

A Year

What joys shall the coming year bring?
The glorious sight of blossom in spring.
Our feathered friends the swallow and lark,
And leisurely ambles in the park.

Children flying their kites on high,
Watch them bob and weave in a clear blue sky.
Crickets chirping when day is done,
After basking in the midsummer sun.

Then the golden gown of Autumn leaves,
Drifting lazily down from majestic trees,
Herald the coming of cold winds that blow,
And bring in their wake a blanket of snow.

Short days, long nights, freezing frosts,
Hardened ground and high fuel costs.
All these things will the coming year bring,
Until, full circle, we return to spring.

Dark Voices

Senses to a height are sharpened.
To dark voices I have harkened.
Will is sapped and strength now drained,
It seems destruction has been ordained.

Darkness comes, robs my sight,
Makes me fearful of the night.
No-one seems to understand.
No longer this torture can I stand.

Now I seek some way to relieve
The dilemma over which I grieve.
For there is no-one to tell of my plight,
And nowhere is safe should I take flight.

Death Throes Of Love

There was no form of defence,
That could protect either you or I,
'Gainst the onslaught, so intense,
That made your love lay down to die.

From whence came the beast
That set our world awry?
And upon emotions did feast,
As your love laid down to die.

A darkness came to dwell,
Within broken hearts to lie.
Drawing compassion into hell,
As your love laid down to die.

Who could but stay sane,
When the will is gone to try?
Or even wish to remain,
To watch your love lay down to die?

Who can bear the coldest days?
Lord knows it is not I.
For e'en now my heart prays,
To lay down with your love to die.

Lonely Hearts

She looks, discerningly, at the glass,
The reflection tells of years gone past.
Counting wrinkles and laughter lines,
That remind her of somewhat earlier times.
A woman in life's early winter,
Married ne'er, still a spinster.
Recalling the many chances missed.

Sitting in her hard earned home,
Glancing at the telephone,
Hoping an old flame may ring
And put an end to her suffering.
But the bell remains all too still,
No-one has phoned and nobody will.
And truth cuts deeply to the bone,
She will spend her last years all alone.
Whilst on the other side of town
A middle aged man is feeling down.
Looking back on his history,
Most of which, to him, is mystery.
Why had he not learned to dance?
Why had he never known romance?
No lady had he in his life,
No lover, fiancée or wife.
Running fingers through thinning pate,
Realising that it is getting late.
Unaware that his 'Miss Right',
Sits and feels the same this night.

The   Blacksmith

Hark the anvil ringing
As his hammer finds its mark.
Hear the old forge singing
As hot coals spit and spark.
Breathe deep the smell of steel
As the blacksmith plies his trade,
Or the acrid odour of annealling
The past creations he has made.
Feel the sweat upon your forehead
Running rivulets down your face.
Such is the smithies homestead,
A most inhospitable place.

Springtime

As I lay me down to think,
'Neath the apple blossom pink,
Living ceiling o'er my head,
Underneath me green grass bed.

All about warm breezes blowing,
Undulating rich blooms growing.
All is silent save the sound
Of songbirds that in the trees abound.

Wisp of cloud in bright blue sky
Floats above the place I lie.
Sunbeams filter through leafy ceiling.
Only springtime can conjure this feeling.

Autumn's Gift

Gaze into the river deep,
Observe dewdrops from the willow weep
And fall silently on their journey down
To mingle with the current and drown.

Autumn leaves also descend
With their own kind below to blend.
A colourful blanket 'pon the ground,
Lying still without a sound.

There to feel the chill winds blow,
The golden gown begins to flow.
Abstract patterns therein created,
As each leaf, in turn, is undulated.

Coming to rest on the river to float,
Carried downstream like a miniature boat,
On an endless voyage out to sea,
For all time lost, but forever free.

My Friend

Dark clouds loom within my mind,
Making my eyes to beauty blind.
Crushing joy with its oppression,
Driving me deeper into depression.

"Fight on, fight on" my tortured mind cries,
But a lack of courage my heart belies.
The darkness increases, its thickness so dense,
My mind and heart races, my fear is intense.

Robbing from me God's gift of sight,
Turning the brightest day into the blackest night.
Drawing from within me my life's last breath.
Leaving nothing to hope for but the sting of death.

But the dread abates and there is courage again,
A force that penetrates the barrier of pain.
That leaves me calm, at peace, so serene,
A friend stands beside me, silent, unseen.

A guardian angel at my shoulder stands,
To help me and guide me taking my hand.
Leading me through like an avenging wraith,
Suddenly I'm aware that my friend is Faith.

The Beast Within

Black is the colour of the beast
That creeps at night with stealth.
Who upon healthy minds doth feast
Robbing logic and mental health.

Unseen, intangible unholy parasite,
That in savage, coldblooded sessions,
Attacks the brain come dark of night,
Banishing sanity to the pit of depression.

In the darkest corner of your mind it resides,
The beast that can turn a genius into a fool.
Come the daylight it runs to its hide,
But in the dreaded darkness it rules.

Is it immortal, this creature of the night?
Or can it get dragged from whence it doth dwell,
And be brought out into the bright daylight,
To be banished, forever, to hell.

Tragedy

He wanders, lost, the empty grounds,
Oblivious to the sights and sounds.
Ignorant of cold winds blowing,
Unaware that it is snowing.

Slippered feet, through snowflakes falling,
Trudge away from voices calling.
Moving on, with measured tread,
Toward the iron gates ahead.

Through the gates, flung open wide,
Steps onto the road outside.
Hearing not the screeching wheels,
One brief instant of pain he feels.

Ambulance speeding, siren loud,
Weaving through gathering crowd.
Staring faces, no word spoken,
Watching motionless body broken.

From the body lifeforce fleeting,
Hurries toward Heavenly greeting.
Wonderful place to think again,
Nevermore to suffer pain.

Nature's Way (Nightmare Scenario)

Open fields for miles and miles,
Unfettered, no walls nor fences or stiles.
Nature's way, open plan,
Undefiled by human hand.

Creatures flew, ran wild and crawled,
Unbound and free, not caged or walled.
The land itself, that too, was free.
All God's creations knew liberty.

This was the way it all began,
And continued until the arrival of man.
But mankind came, 'civilization' grew,
Amassed more knowledge to that he knew.

Soon moved from caves to huts of wood,
Built crude walls and thought them good.
So came about the fateful day,
When mankind undermined nature's way.

The land he tried to captivate,
By wall or fence and five-bar gate.
All too soon came his greatest feat,
For then man invented concrete.

His concrete jungle soon did spread,
But mankind counted not the creatures dead.
Steel towers rose up into the skies,
Whilst man was deaf to nature's cries.

With each of mankind's endeavours finished,
Another species of God's diminished.
None too soon came man's swansong,
Nuclear power and the "bomb".

Too late did man come to decide
That he was commiting suicide.
Felt each day ever more distressed,
Waiting for the "button" to be pressed.

A world in turmoil, all went bad,
Curdled by mankind gone mad.
Never bothering to count the cost,
Man unleashed the holocaust.

Concrete crumbled into dust,
Great steel towers nought but rust.
With the last man drawing his final breath,
Just like a lemming racing to his death.

But mother nature is surely strong,
Would not let this emptiness last for long.
Once more the skies will fill with rain,
And lush green grass shall grow again.

Open fields for miles and miles,
Unfettered, no walls nor fences or stiles.
Nature's way, open plan.
Undefiled by human hand.

The Enemy Above (A Day At Heathrow?)

Hear the mighty engines scream as the awesome powers rise.
And the endless squadrons of silver birds take unto the skies.
See the great clouds of pollution falling all over the ground.
Protect your delicate eardrums from the loud unearthly
                                                sounds.
As jumbo jets and Concordes swiftly burn up all their fuels,
And mankind depletes earth's energy, the incompetent, near
                                                sighted fools.

69

Just Another Year

The warmer days of summer haze
Have slipped into the past.
And frosty nights, now winter bites,
Are upon us all at last.

The fifth of November, a night to remember,
That, too, has passed away.
Christmas, a time of good cheer will soon be here,
Though it's nearly yesterday.

Time quickly flies, as the old year dies,
And thrashes all in vain.
For, all too soon, comes that magic book,
Spring shall be born again.

Who Will Remember?

When I'm dead, my body rotten,
Will these verses be forgotten?
Or will they rouse a curious mind,
In some far reaching distant time?

Could the workings of my hand,
Survive the trickle of destiny's sand?
When my mind is, finally, free,
Shall I be remembered in history?

Probably not, why should they care,
About some historic archaic despair?
So my warnings no-one will hear,
Though the world is filling with fear.

As my mind is clouding with dread,
With the horrors rising inside my head,
One thing is certain through the haze,
Life is stepping out of phase.

The 'Way'

Through the streets of life we wander,
Some to act others to ponder.
A few to lead the many led,
Harken the words the wise men have said.

There are also a number of fools,
Evil dictators and several ghouls.
Then callous, murdering villains,
Who prey upon defenceless young children.

Adulterers that whole families break,
Unbalanced minds that their own lives take.
Thieves that steal as a labour,
People who, secretly, covet their neighbour.

Satanists who idolise hell,
And may be sent there to forever dwell.
Worshippers of images craven
Also, by God, shall be forsaken.

Incestuous folk who their own do know,
These, and others, to hades go.
The ten commandments have all been broken.
No wonder the prophets have not spoken.

Proclaiming the coming a second time,
Of Jesus of Nazareth, Son of the Divine.
Whence mankind hath taken God inside,
Only then shall He here again reside.

Summertime

Luxuriate in the splendour of summer days,
Leisurely bathe in the warm sun's rays.
Feel the heat at the height of noon.
Enjoy summers evenings coming soon.

When crickets chirp their evensong,
Nights are warm and days are long.
Partake of blackberries 'pon wild brambles
As you wend your way on summer ambles.

Rest your feet in a cool stream flowing.
Count the variety of flowers there growing.
Returning home when the sun's heat does fade,
Quenching your thirst with chilled lemonade.

Thank God For The Samaritans

I stumbled, lonely, through the town,
Heart sunk low, spirits slumped down.
Inhaling the poison from cars and vans,
When I happened upon the Samaritans,

I gulped again at the toxic air,
Mused a moment 'pon my own despair.
Read the sign, swallowed my pride,
And, hand on door, stepped inside.

I was welcomed and led into a private room,
Where I was able to unload my burden of gloom,
And when I left 'twas with the trace of a smile,
For I had been comforted for just a short while.

A Place By The Sea

Silence falls heavy across the empty bay,
The multitude of tourists have all gone away.
The pier now untrodden by endless hordes of feet,
And the tide has long washed footprints from the beach.

This is just a ghost town when the year grows old.
No-one walks the promenade for it is too cold.
Hotel rooms are vacant, the arcades all closed down.
Search for somewhere open, but nothing can be found.

Even hardened seagulls seem lacking in all cheer,
Few, indeed, in the winter months, even venture near.
The last fragment of litter blows, lonely, across the street,
Carries on across the sands until the tide it meets.

Engulfed by an unseen wave and carried out to sea,
Leaving nothing moving in this deserted town but me.
And I, too, must move on and away from this depressing place,
Which seems to have been discarded by the entire human race.

'Pon The Table

Red and yellow, pink and green,
The most wonderous sight ever I've seen.
Describe I would, if I were but able,
The splendour of flowers 'pon the table.

Rose and tulip, orchid and carnation,
All add their beauty to this decoration.
Breathe deeply of their natural perfume,
As it permeates throughout the room.

I thank God for all the hours
That I spend among the flowers.
Such a shame how soon they die,
Becoming repulsive to mine eye.

Trains

Feel the ground atremble
As the sleepers take the strain
Of a hundred tons of cargo
Drawn by mighty diesel train.
Taking coal to power stations,
Iron ore to foundries,
A hundred different materials
To a thousand factories.

The early morning milk train
Collects the evening mail,
Delivers morning papers
Newsagents put out for sale.
Intercity express trains
Quickly thunder past,
Carrying commuters
Who all seem to be 'first class',

Each one wearing bowler,
Umbrella rolled so neat,
Pinstripe suit, Financial Times,
Black leather shoes on feet.
Going to the 'City'
To deal in stocks and shares.
Making million dollar fortunes
About which no-one cares.

Working in plush offices,
Strictly nine-'til-five.
Struggling in a cut-throat world,
Just trying to survive.
Eight hours at the desk,
Time for home again,
Like a plague of locusts,
Descending on the trains.

Return Me To Dreamland

Fire and brimstone in my nostrils burned,
Gastric juices in my stomach churned.
Flames of hell into my body lanced,
Whilst, to a tune of death, the demons danced.

Beelzebub came forth, horns all afire,
As he approached hades flames grew higher.
The demons ceased their dance of death,
And I could feel Satan's fiery breath.

He looked at me as one he knew well,
I was to become a sacrifice to hell.
Mighty trident, with prongs sharply pointed,
Aimed at me, one annointed.

The Devil hurled it straight to my chest,
I remember the pain though I forget the rest.
For 'twas in that instant I woke from my dream
Only to wish I were back whence I'd been.

Christmas Cheer?

Christmas time is here once more.
The towns are crowded as before.
People who complained yesterday
Complain once more about low pay.
Same thing happens every year
Still buy presents, oh, so dear.
Discontentment o'er times so hard.
But still they bash the credit card.
A revered event once idolised,
Now laid to waste and commercialised.

You're Gone

Like a cancerous growth inside my heart,
My love grew more each day,
From that moment we did part,
And I watched you walk away.

At first I knew not where to start,
Nor the price I'd have to pay,
Or how my entire soul could smart,
When you said you would not stay.

I had to learn across the years,
How to become a better man,
And swam through the oceans of tears,
To get to where I am.

But not enough to quell the fears
I tried smothering when I began,
And now, at last, the final curtain rears,
For I have done everything I can.

A Brief Holiday

Imagine Egypt in the heart of noon,
The shifting sands of each vast dune.
Picture the pyramids, the banks of the Nile.
Ponder the Sphinx and linger a while.

Consider the triangle, a pet hobby of mine,
Explore it and Bermuda, land of sunshine.
As I gaze o'er the oceans so blue,
Far across the sea to horizons new.

Watching the waves break on the silver sand,
And wonder about some other distant land.
Florida, Miami, the Big Apple too,
So many places and so much to do.

Perhaps the Bahamas should be my next trip,
A first class cruise on a luxury ship.
Oh, I have been everywhere it seems,
Such a shame it was all in my dreams.

A Protest

On a cold and lonely doorstep,
At the first light of dawn.
A woman places a cardboard box,
Inside is her first born.

The scribbled, misspelt message
With it tragically reads,
"Please look after my baby,
Give him the love he needs".

The government does nothing,
Despite the hue and cry,
And at the fund starved hospital,
The unfortunate infant dies.

As, realistically, I look at life,
It is then hardly surprising,
That, day by day, the suicide rate,
Alarmingly goes on rising.

Only At The Full Moon

The first night of the full moon,
Every window is shut tight.
Villagers will retire soon,
No-one ventures out at night.

Not in the moonshine,
Not when it is in this phase,
People only stir at daytime
For these three unholy days.

When the evening starts afalling,
The shadows long upon the ground,
Then it starts its calling,
An inhuman, bloodcurdling sound.

Travellers stop at daylight,
Many across the years,
Those that camped at night,
At full moon, always disappeared.

For here the werewolf roams,
Throughout the countryside,
And those who left their homes,
At full moon, have always died.

Throats torn out by the beast,
A creature half wolf, half man.
Who upon human flesh doth feast,
At the full moon whene'er it can.

So make fast your dwelling,
When the full moon shines.
For there is no foretelling
On whom he may next dine.

Who Is Innocent When The Killing Starts?

He had not started this bloody war,
Nor, truly, knew what he was fighting for.
Just obeying orders as a warrior should,
Each soldier believing that they fought for 'good'.

The same old phrase "good against bad",
Where was the good in this world gone mad?
"Who was the better when all had slain?"
So many questions now tormented his brain.

Ears painfully numb with the rifles' report,
And the whistling bullets of the enemy's retort.
Firing his Lee Enfield, round after round,
Watching, revulsed, as each target went down.

Awaiting the order, at last to advance,
Though the thousands before had never a chance.
Cut down before even a yard could be gained,
Ever more men replacing the slain.

Then darkness came, 'oh, blessed night',
Removing the carnage from his sight.
But all about he could hear men screaming,
Whether he was wakeful or fitfully dreaming.

"Fix bayonets", he heard the commander cry,
And, wondering had the time come to die?
Advanced under night's cloak of black,
Striving to conceal a daring attack.

Steadily crossing no-mans-land,
Everything going as the generals had planned.
When flares burst brightly and surprise was lost,
The advancing troops bearing a horrendous cost.

Caught 'twixt the lines, nowhere to run,
Nowhere to hide nought could be done.
Confusion and doubt where discipline had been,
Throughout that nightmare fear reigned supreme.

With gunfire ahead and mortar behind,
A battalion of infantrymen were blind.
Not knowing, now, where they should be,
The foe sending them headlong into eternity.

79

Another flare flashed and split the night,
Exposing the allies in their infernal plight.
Mortar shells exploding again and again,
Men struggling helplessly, dying or maimed.

He stumbled on, face beaded with sweat,
Trying, vainly, to achieve the task they'd been set.
Unaware of the bullets bringing men down,
Long since past hearing the shells all around.

Barely conscious when he, too, fell,
Brought low by the force of an explosive shell.
Clambering to return to his feet once more,
Cursing the pain and denouncing the war.

The Disease

'Tis an evil existence that mortal man does lead,
Fired by ambition and fuelled by burning greed.
Many wars, for obscure reasons, he has fought.
To the sacred value of life has given little thought.

Now he contemplates upon a solution,
To damage caused by his own pollution.
As an 'intelligent' being he has scant sense,
To creatures extinct has no conscience.

Drilling for oil and digging for coal,
Pondering never 'pon his mortal soul.
His effect on nature must surely be
The final curtain falling on his destiny.

For he has made God's earth so obscene
With his infernal internal combustion machines.
Coming into a world so clean and pure,
Man has become a disease, but what is the cure?

Who Knows?

My father, in his thoughts, may be just about me,
Then again, it's possible that he just may be,
Looking on the dim side, never on the bright,
Seeing only darkness, observing not the light.

Knowing not the pain that dwells within my heart,
Which, each and every hour, tears my soul apart.
Never understanding the turmoil inside my mind,
Emotions that distort logic of any kind.

Leaving me confused, knowing not which way to turn,
Calculating thoughtwaves laid waste by that for which I yearn.
Letting not my programmed logic eradicate the pain,
Of a broken heart that I suffer once again.

Mayhap I'll always suffer, perhaps that is my fate,
Looking back I notice the years are getting late.
The more I dwell upon it the clearer it seems to me,
That a solitude existence is all that frames my destiny.

Dogs Of War

The battle was hard and, oh, so cruel,
No prisoners would be taken.
The hounds of war began to drool,
And mercy was forsaken.

No white flags would be flown.
No quarter asked nor given.
As ever nearer came the drone
Of war machines hard driven.

'Tis over now though older we're grown.
Older, wiser and now shriven.
Waiting for compassion to be shown
To know that we are forgiven.

The Follies Of War

I have stood among the ghouls,
Counting the graves of so many fools,
Who gave up their lives, and even more,
For a 'cause', and that cause was war.

How many men have spilled their blood,
Their mangled bodies stamped into the mud?
How many men have suffered in vain?
And how many times must it happen again?

Countless rounds the soldiers reload,
Countless shells the cannons explode,
And countless times the bayonet cuts,
Spilling untold quantities of blood and guts.

But when the fighting is over and done
Bigger fools such as I look on
And ponder why is man so unkind,
And why the governments are so blind?

Fighting The Night

Count the seconds ticking away,
Until, at last, comes break of day.
Demons of thought yet to fight,
That only attack in the dark of night.

Then it is finally over and done,
The enemy repelled by the rising sun.
Time to recuperate from conflicts' pain,
Ready to fight when it begins again.

The casualty rate grows steadily higher,
And weary warriors start to tire.
The future looks to be, oh, so stark,
Awaiting the onslaught again at dark.

Introduction

Virgin paper I violate,
In an effort to create,
Some piece that stands the test of time,
And be, perhaps, savoured like vintage wine.

Conjuring visions of the sun's warm rays,
On cold and overcast wintry days.
Or chill your blood in the heat of noon,
Play on your heartstrings to make you swoon.

To touch the emotions I shall aspire,
Take you from laughter to heated ire.
Then bring you back to earth again,
If I can do these things I shall achieve my aim.

The Fireman

His day is not a happy one, he knows what to expect,
The only difference is where they will need him next.
He wonders what sort of danger 'this' day will bring.
How many people will endure the endless suffering?

He cannot count the number of victims he has saved,
Nor the raging infernos that, head-on, he has braved.
The helpless people he has rescued from a burning room,
And the amount of toxic smoke that he has to consume.

A highly trained professional doing his job as best he can.
Where would we all be without him, that fearless fireman.
The next time you see a house with windows all ablaze,
Remember to offer the firefighter his hard earned worthy
                                            praise.

The Guilt Of Innocence

It was not he who begat the fight,
With his back to the wall could not take flight.
When the mugger threatened his very life,
Ever advancing, wielding the knife.

These thoughts had haunted him for three long days,
Until memory, itself, became a shadowy haze.
And now he stood, still suffering from shock,
Not the victim, but the accused, in the dock.

He had not meant to cause such harm,
But sought only to, the assailant, disarm.
Now he, numbly, asked the question 'why?'
Is it illegal to wish not to die?

In the court, the charge being read,
He could not answer, so filled with dread.
"Manslaughter", the word rang loud in his ears,
Conjuring untold visions of diabolical fears.

Self-preservation is wrong it would seem,
Or would he awaken from a horrific dream?
The question he asked himself, time after time,
"Is self-defence such an abominable crime?"

It was kill or be killed, he could never win.
It was either die or commit a terrible sin.
He'd tried to coerce the attacker, but failed,
Now, instead of his assailant, he would be jailed.

The doubts came again, the same as before,
Whatever he did he'd fall foul of the law.
The sentence read, he looked the judge in the eye,
But the only word to escape his lips was "Why?"

Wintertime

Winter has arrived, the snow is drifting down,
Covering the countryside with an ermine gown.
Little robin redbreasts have come back once more,
Nesting in the honeysuckle just as they did before.

Naked trees upon the horizon white with snow and frost,
Seem so stark and rigid now their leaves they've lost.
The guttering is hanging heavy with icicles once again,
And freezing air makes crystal patterns on the window pane.

Blackbirds defend the sparrows that they, too, may feed,
And not be chased away by the starlings in their greed.
The bluetits hang and nibble on a fatty bacon rind,
Whilst pigeons and thrushes eat what scraps they find.

For this is the winter plight of our feathered friends.
The hard, and often fruitless, search for food that never ends.
If more people took the time to scatter a little seed or bread,
Winter would be less harsh, for these birds would be better fed.

* * *

So those are the poems submitted. I have been especially
careful to make sure that I have reproduced them faithfully.
What was the reaction to them from our would-be publishers?

John Burke sent 'Roberts' a "report from an independent
editor" on behalf of **Avon Books**, signed by A. E. Rawlinson
which stated "I particularly liked the closely constructed yet
explosively apocalyptic language of 'Enemy Above', and
the thought-provoking sense of futility engendered by
'Who Is Innocent When The Killing Starts' . . . whatever the
intention Roberts hits home from every angle . . . I feel that

this book will be a great source of inspiration for groups and individuals alike." The covering letter stated that they would be, "pleased to publish your poems . . . in hardback with dust jacket for £2,400 or £2,000 with a semi–stiff laminated cover . . . In either case the sum is payable in four instalments." Much was made in their letter of their marketing advice – W H Smith being mentioned by name.

Avon Books had supplied me with a copy of one of their books and I asked my Printer if he would cost out a similar book of 48 pages for me, with in each case, a good profit margin for himself. 200 copies would cost £661 and 500 copies £892.

Lisa Kirkpatrick for **Dorrance Publishing** first wrote to tell me I'd have to allow, "between 45 and 60 days for our editors in our Pittsburgh office in America to review your work." While I was waiting to hear I read through in more detail their 'Author's Guide To Subsidy Publishing'. They offered three basic service packages:

1) To produce and promote a book, within their *Traditional Subsidy Publishing Scheme*, deciding the book specifications themselves, within a defined budget. They normally print 1,000 copies of the book and guaranteed to keep the book in stock and on their list for a minimum two years, also to produce up to 500 direct mail 'pieces' announcing the book.

Their literature states that few of their publications receive national review, but that they will send out publicity releases written by their own promotion staff and approximately 100 publicity releases and jackets are sent to wholesalers, distributors and jobbers.

2) For those who prefer not to have Dorrance's limited promotional service, wishing to handle their own marketing, Dorrance provide a *Self–Publishing* service, manufacturing a specific number of books under the author's own imprint and to the author's own specifications while working

closely with the author to produce an "appropriate and appealing volume." But with this service you are obviously then responsible for your own warehousing and distribution and thus all the books are sent to you on completion.

The 3rd service they offer is *Limited Edition or Private Printing* which although similar to the self–publishing programme, caters for those who are "essentially seeking a specific number of books for private use." The publication package for this service is the same as for self–publishing, both having a minimum run of 250 copies.

To price against American publications is not simple, Dorrance had sent us a book which was 230 x 150mm, a size that fits no known standard English size envelope – the standard A5 size being 210 x 148mm. My Printer costed against a similar book, but to a standard A5 size, which came out at £619 for 250 copies, £854 for 500, and £1,225 for 1,000 copies.

We still have the problem for comparison of American costs being different to British costs, British published books not having to carry shipment costs from the US to the UK – from that point alone it would seem somewhat illogical to go to the States to have your book published – and the public interest in the USA for books of (in the main) totally unknown UK poets is an unknown factor.

Peter Nicholas, Director of **Arthur H. Stockwell** wrote to say that he had carefully assessed the work and would "advise 40 poems were enclosed not 48 with the (listed) poems repeated." He offered, after a payment of £2,361 from me, "to bind 200 copies of an initial edition of up to 3,500 copies . . . priced at £4.99 a copy." I would receive "12 complimentary copies and could purchase additional copies at £2.00 each." I would also receive "99p per copy royalty for copies sold in the UK," though it was pointed out that I would not receive a royalty on "books purchased by you at the special price." A special one colour leaflet solely advertising my book would be produced and sent out in their usual mailings.

A hardback book (glued not stitched) was sent from Stockwell. My Printer priced a 48 page version of this at £1,889 for 200 copies and £2,315 for 500.

J Lyons of **Excalibur** sent a Literary Panel, Poetry Editorial Report, signed by Ed Beerbohm, which suggested that "the author competently handles a wide range of subjects, issues and emotions . . . rhyme and cadence are employed to great effect . . . a very attractive poetic style," at the same time pointing out that 'Roberts' had in fact only submitted 32 poems, not the claimed 48 and listed those duplicated. J Lyons' covering letter offered to "accept your work for publication on our usual standard subsidy and royalties scheme" which they were prepared to do, "in view of the editor's recommendation," at a total cost of £1,960 in four stages – "£560 on signing the contract. £450 on approving the editing. £500 on approving the typesetting and £450 when the work is completed." The offer included, "royalties of 40% to the author until the entire subsidy is recovered and thereafter 20% which represents a profit element." From this, the booklet *Help* received from both Excalibur and Adelphi stresses that the author will not be charged for their marketing cost. I have not been able to get a sample book from Excalibur.

Perhaps J Lyons of **Adelphi** appreciated that both companies had been sent the same poems. Leastways we've had no further reply from him. I would however say that in 1991 an NPF subscriber received a letter from J West (Chief Executive) of Adelphi saying that her work "had a quality that set it apart," which then introduced her to their "partnership between publisher and author wherein both contribute and both share the profits," and that although a subsidy was required from the author, "this is amply compensated by the size of the royalties which are about double those offered by other publishers." (I quote J West's letter of March 27th 1991). At that time I rang Adelphi and told the man who answered the phone that I had a 40 page poetry book to publish. "What's it going to cost me," I asked. "£1,900," the voice answered. "For how many copies," I asked. "100," he said.

No doubt since 1991 both number of copies and cost of contribution will have altered – I give you the information above only in view of the fact that J Lyons has failed to comment on the 40+ poems sent to him by 'Locke'.

Anthony Phillips, Editorial Director of **Pentland Press**, had originally written to say that "the manuscript of poems, upon first glance, appears quite impressive," having asked for an "author's contribution of at least £3,500 with an average being in the region of £5,500."

A four page *Reader's Report* from Brian Wheeler on behalf of Pentland Press was sent to 'Roberts' in which he says "The poet addresses with insight and diversity an impressive number of contemporary concerns . . . to summarise, the collection in its entirety will surely cause the reader to think and feel deeply about the current state of society . . ." and goes on to say "Both the style and subject matter displayed will appeal to a potentially wide market, and therefore I have no hesitation in recommending this collection for publication." The covering letter signed by Anthony Phillips offered to publish 1,000 copies for £4,176, at the same time explaining how this money would be regained through sales of the book. This letter also pointed out that "as you will no doubt have deduced from our Book List, we are selective in the poetry which we include, primarily because we are only prepared to accept works which we consider to have the potential to be successful." According to Anthony's letter, Pentland would (usually) sell fifty percent of the books, the other fifty percent being sold through the book trade.

Anthony subsequently wrote to both 'Locke' and 'Roberts' suggesting they had both sent in the same poems and mentioning copyright laws – proving that 'Pentland Press' and 'Editorial Office W' were one and the same company at different offices.

He sent copies of two books. According to my Printer the cost of 1,000 copies of each would have been respectively, £1,250 and £1,290 – again in both instances costed to leave a good profit margin for himself.

The Book Guild's Carol Biss, Editorial Director, wrote to say that they would take 'Roberts' poetry to publish – The Book Guild had previously reported that "it looks interesting."

In her first paragraph Carol Biss went to some pains to explain that "where poetry is concerned, regardless of content, it would be unlikely that you would get much return" and that "we cannot make books sell . . . we would not like you to come in with us with any unrealistic view of publishing." She offered a case bound book with gold blocking and a well designed and dignified wrapper 216 x 135mm with a first print run of 500 copies and a contribution from 'Roberts' of £5,200 towards costs. In return for which he would receive 30% of the full retail price as royalty which is "the equivalent of 80% of the net receipts/revenue: this is more than twice the normal royalty rate in publishing." If 'Roberts' paid in one go 50 free copies would be received. If instead he paid in three instalments spread over approximately a year, he would receive 20 free copies. Marketing of the book would be through the library cataloguing list and The Book Guild's sales representatives "who cover the whole country and telephone calls would also be made."

When I pressed her to send us a copy of their internal 'evaluation' against which they had decided to publish, Carol Biss wrote back (returning the poems) saying "we are a publishing service and the critical difference between mainstream and us is that we are not choosing manuscripts on judgement of commercial success." She goes on to say that "as an author's money is involved it would be wrong, as in the case of the vanity press, of giving you glowing readers reports that you base your decision to publish on."

The Book Guild had also (like Stockwell) sent me a hardback book (glued not stitched) and again my Printer was asked to price a 48 page version of it. £2,668 for 200 copies, £3,458 for 500.

Having found that **Quest Publishing** had ceased trading, at least from the address given, I was surprised when it was two whole months after the original posting that we received the poems back from the Post Office marked 'gone away'.

John Thorpe on behalf of **Regency Press** wrote to thank 'Locke' for sending him the 48 poem collection but that there were more than one copy of some so "there are 28 in all, which would be about right for a 32–page booklet," and enclosed a sample. This is a "private edition," he wrote, "so all 600 copies will be sent to you when it is printed and bound. The cost is £500, half payable when you give instructions to proceed and the balance when copies are ready." It should be noted that the sample of what I would receive for my money was an A6 (half the size of an A5) booklet.

My Printer costed this example at £485 for 600 copies.

Ross Stanton for **Janus** Publishing Co said "in our opinion you have a true poetic impulse and we are pleased to accept your work for publication under our standard co–partnership and royalty terms" going on to say that they suggested a "semi–stiff laminated one sided Art cover printed two colour. Perfect bound. Format Demy 8vo/A5." Janus only required an investment of £1,960 in three stages – £653.33 on signing a contract; £653.33 on approving the typesetting; £653.34 when the work is completed. Ross then went on to give details of their substantial marketing procedure – through trade outlets, library cataloguing, circulation of booksellers. "Markets which your title would be best suited to will be carefully selected." He further sent copies of three hand written letters of thanks, with the addresses and telephone numbers masked out. Here my Printer costed a similar book at £619 for 200 copies, £854 for 500 copies and £1,225 for 1,000 copies.

Derek Stockwell, Director of **Merlin Books Ltd**, 40 East Street, Braunton, Devon EX33 2EA tel: 0271 812117, whose name I had come across after my initial newspaper search, sent 'Locke' details of their *Alternative Bookplan* which involved binding batches of 200 copies of the small A5 booklet which the 24 poems sent (there had been duplications) would make or, if preferred (option two), to have each poem printed on a separate page and have four preliminary pages – i.e. a 36 page book. Each offered up to 1,250 copies in batches of 200 returning £737 (at a cost of £721) and £875 (at a cost of £867) respectively in royalties to cover outlay. In each case the poet would be sent 12 complimentary copies of the book. With the first proposal, additional copies after the initial 200 would be sent at £1.47 up to 1,250 copies and £1.77 thereafter. With the second option up to 1,250 for £1.75 and £2.10 thereafter.

My Printer costed 200 copies of the 36 page book at £578, the 48 page book £607 with 1,250 copies of the first at £1,365, the second at £1,422. Merlin also sent a copy of a more expensively produced book (115gsm matt coated pages with a full colour photo reproduction included) which for 200 copies, was priced at £946 for 36 page and £1,002 for 48 page. For 1,250 copies the cost was £1,970 and £2,095 respectively. Merlin also stated that although they couldn't guarantee sales of any book, they would undertake "to promote the sale of the book by mailing to selected distributors including library suppliers. We also send copies to the Review editors of a selection of suitable journals."

On behalf of **Minerva**, I received an 'Editorial Evaluation' signed by Ann Austin – reader, and 'passed' by Arthur Thorndyke, Editorial Director, which claimed that "these are pleasing, quite formally structured poems . . . I believe that they could find a readership among those who care about form . . . the work is quite strongly imagist . . . I was rather reminded of the fine work of Hilda Doolittle[1], an under rated follower of Ezra Pound." The covering letter suggested a "partnership of £1,800 on the part of 'Roberts' in four equal payments, with a royalty of 45% until the outlay had been recovered and thereafter, 22.5% – around twice the usual percentage paid by other publishers." Once the book had been published they would "with our international marketing contacts begin the work of promoting your book. Review copies are sent to various publications, mail order is sometimes used, the book is entered in the booksellers' list, and it is placed with UK and overseas distribution networks." On the phone Mr Thorndyke told me that 'Roberts' would "get 30 free copies and could then buy others at 40% of the list price" – they would, he said, print "a few hundred copies initially."

[1](author's note) *Hilda Doolittle (1886–1961). American Imagist poet known as HD who came to London in 1911. Married English writer Richard Aldington in 1913 and divorced him in 1937, subsequently living in Geneva until she died. In my opinion the poetry of 'Roberts' bears no comparison whatsoever with that of HD, either in structure or in quality.*

Finally, an advert that was found too late to be sent either the initial 3 poems or the 40 . . . **Kudos Books Ltd** of 1 Russell Chambers, The Piazza, Covent Garden, London WC2E 8AA tel: 071 836 1908, run by Mary and Peter Harrison. I received a letter from Mary on their behalf detailing the cost of 200 copies of a 48 page A5 poetry book at £486. The cost was payable in 6 instalments of £81 each. The letter goes on to paragraph their various services – "dealing directly with major buyers, wholesalers and libraries as well as selling through their team of sales representatives. Endeavouring to sell paperback, film, television and video rights. Searching out each book's 'hidden treasure' [i.e. its marketing potential] from which a press release is prepared and sent to newspapers and   magazines."

All of which sounds very much aimed at the prose, rather than poetry market.

There is also the offer to "professionally assess every manuscript from which a comprehensive critique will be prepared free of charge."

My Printer agreed that their costing of the book was a fair enough price for what was offered, but from the paper weight suggested, there was a distinct fear of 'ghosting through' (lettering showing through from one page to another). It would also have led to the book being too thin to have a substantial enough spine on which the title and poet's name should appear, something upon which bookshops are inclined to insist. After further discussion with Peter Harrison about both the paper weight and marketing I received another letter from Mary in which she quoted for a similar book but with 115gm paper at £561 for 200 copies, or on the budget plan, six payments of £93.50 (my Printer again agreed that this was as near spot-on as to make no odds) and included Peter's thoughts on marketing which I reproduce below:

1. Arrange interview with Arts Editor of local newspaper to

discuss poetry in general, the history of poetry, poetry groups in county, favourite poems. Endeavour to have one of the poems from a book published in the newspaper. We would mention local bookshops where the book can be purchased and give the address for mail order sales.

2. Arrange the same type of interview for local radio arts programme.

3. Contact local poetry groups to have author give readings from the book. Give details of where book can be purchased.

4. Arrange further poetry readings to Art Groups, Drama/Operatic/Writing Societies and Circles.

5. Confer with author regarding further ideas and marketing strategies.

I shall be interested to hear from anyone submitting a poetry manuscript to this company.

* * *

So there we have it. For all of you who said this exercise should be done, what have we learned?

. . . that all those publishers who can afford to mount large advertising programmes are in publishing as a Business with a capital 'B', to make a profit and are not philanthropic – but that's the function of all businesses.

. . . that their prices are geared to the massive overheads they claim to have to service – not only in advertising but also in staff levels – and not in any way to making *you* a profit. Again, nothing unusual there.

. . . that each offers a marketing and publication service which each claims to be second to none. Well you would hardly expect any to heap praise on another's service at its own expense!

. . . that anyone may offer a service at whatever price they feel the market will bear. Why not? It is after all up to the potential customer whether a particular offer is taken up or not and it is

95

virtually impossible to check (with many businesses, not just those in publishing) whether a promised sales drive has actually been attempted. With companies in many spheres of the service industries you have to take on trust the service offered – hoping the 'proof of the pudding' proves the promises have been honoured. However, as is often the case, you only discover this after you have parted with a large sum of money for which there is no legal statute to help you reclaim, should you feel you have been misled or poorly advised.

Nothing illegal, unusual, immoral or fattening, in any of that. So what, if anything, *is* wrong or unfair in the way one, or some, or any of these companies have shown they operate?

To say that an appreciation of poetry is 'subjective' is of course over–simplistic nonsense. A tightly written, well disciplined, well crafted poem, that says something of interest to the reader and not just to the poet's own navel or his auntie, will be recognised as a good well written poem by anyone with the slightest awareness of poetry – one may not like what the poem says, or how it says it, but one has to acknowledge it as well written. The weakly crafted, poorly written verse full of archaic language, the over–obvious, the banal, the twee and the forced rhyme, is recognised as simply poor boring verse by anyone with half an ear for poetic cadences.

There is of course between those two extremes, what I call 'journeyman poetry'. That poetry which may hold the attention of one editor and not another. Be considered interesting by one reader and not another. Be thought of as well written by one but not another – here there *can* be a claim for 'subjectivity'.

It would have been pointless for me to have submitted well crafted poetry on the grounds that there would have been nothing good said about it that could have been challenged. Equally if I had submitted 'journeyman poetry' it could have been argued that almost anything said in appraisal, could, in someone's eyes, have been acceptable.

No, it had to be out–and–out poorly crafted work that was submitted so that any comment by the publishers could be fairly balanced against the poem's true poetic worth. At the same time the three poems were sent to the above addresses they were also shown to and read by a number of poetry editors and poets whose opinion I respected and knew to be respected by the poetry world in general. I could find not one who would have given any one of the poems house–room, or who did anything other than smile at them as examples of the weakest of poor, ill constructed verse.

The poems were recognised by the poetry world for what they were. And don't forget, after the best part of 30 years working with poetry and poets and having been a successful, broadcast and published poet myself, I had constructed the three poems – so I should know their worth as poetry, if anyone!

But the person submitting work to advertisers in the daily press is seldom someone with a proven poetic knowledge and ability. More often, the aspiring poet has little experience of the poetry world. So, if someone to whom he has written – found advertising in a well renowned national paper – tells him his work is good, there's a bit of a rude awakening (and some heavy and indignant flak for the poor poetry magazine editor) when the same work is sent out into the poetry world, only to find it isn't considered well enough or interestingly enough written to warrant publication. "But so–and–so said . . !" is often the indignant cry.

Why then, you will ask, do these publishers, or rather their editorial staff, wax lyrical in their reports on verse which to one hundred percent of the *poetry* world is less than acceptable?

It would be discourteous to allege that any of the

reports were motivated by a wish to entice the potential customer into believing the poetry they had submitted more worthy of publication than was perhaps the truth and hence, that they would be more liable to pay to have it published.

It would of course be mischievous of me were I to suggest that perhaps *some* of those who write these appraisals have not the slightest jot of poetic awareness in their entire bodies and that their comments *could,* if that *were* the case, simply be income motivated?

It would be uncharitable to suggest the claim that the initial outlay will/may be recouped from sales of the book is perhaps, just a little . . . exaggerated. I leave you, the reader, to do the sums – divide the average number of copies promised by the amount of the payment demanded and that will tell you for what each and every one of those copies (not just some of, or a percentage of, but the total) must sell, if you are to break even and get back your initial outlay . . . ah! but you may only get 60% or 70% or 75% of sale price in some cases – an even longer and steeper uphill struggle for those returning pennies.

Where some of the companies talk of 'share publishing', or 'a contribution towards', or 'a donation to costs', might someone less charitable than I suggest that it would seem from the amounts requested, this 'share', this 'contribution', this 'donation' to be the total cost plus a healthy profit margin of and for the whole publishing venture?

I would be a coarse fellow indeed were I to suggest that in some cases some of the books might be better produced, a little more of the customer's cash spent on their creation.

Of course a part of the problem (by their own admission) is that most of these companies deal with such a small number of poets as a percentage of their overall annual turnover. Most of the books with which they deal are novels, romances, thrillers or autobiographies.

So they would be seen to be being more fair and open to

their potential (poetic) customers, if they were all to say *"although we are not in a position to comment on the quality of your work,* we would be prepared to undertake publication for £x," and, "you must appreciate that the chance of recouping *other than a very small amount of your original outlay is extremely slight indeed, the chances of making a profit – infinitesimal. Very few people other than your own relations and friends are likely to actually buy and read your verses,"* should be added.

Also, where a company in its correspondence talks of sending copies of a book to the British Museum Library and to the (usually listed) University Libraries – as though doing a service – what they should be saying is that *"by act of Parliament they (as with every other publisher in the UK) have to send a copy of every book published to the British Museum Library and 5 copies of it to the Copyright Receipts Office in London and that it is they who then distribute the books to the University Libraries."*

One thing is very certain. Whatever some of these companies charge for publication and whatever claims they make, many of those they do publish in book form as poets would never find an established poetry magazine or recognised poetry publisher to undertake to publish their work for them – whatever they offered to pay.

You as a reader will be excused expressing sceptical bemusement at some of these publishers' claims where marketing is concerned, when you balance them against the views expressed by many buyers and owners of bookshops in Chapter VI – but that is yet to come.

One may well be able to hawk a novel, romance or thriller around the various bookshops and end up with some orders. The chance of doing the same with a poetry book is marginal to say the least and if you can get a bookshop interested, it will too often wish to take copies only on a 'sale–or–return' basis. Couple that with the minimum 35%–45% discount that any bookshop will require (they are also in Business with a capital 'B') and you perhaps begin to understand that the *selling* of your book is another world altogether.

Don't get me wrong, if you or your publisher can interest your local newspaper and radio in giving you and your book some coverage, or even better a national magazine or newspaper, you may well then find that your local bookshops are willing to take copies – so all is not gloom and doom – you may well sell at least as many as a dozen copies this way!

No, when it comes down to it, the only way you stand a chance of seeing your outlay back is if you have a large family and almost endless list of friends who can be coerced into buying a copy, or if you are famous in some other field. In other words the success of your publication in monetary terms is more often than not down to your own efforts or your own notoriety.

"How many of the companies listed in the previous pages have the expertise, the mechanics or the basic knowledge of the poetry market to market your product successfully, from your pocket's point of view," is not what we are questioning. Their profit does not depend on the sale of copies of your book (marketing), it depended on the profit 'mark–up' on the figure they charged you to publish those copies. If you were to do your own publishing that is one outlay you wouldn't have to cover before you stood a chance of breaking even.

Another phenomenon you may care to consider . . . I invite you (and every other poet I can contact in the whole of the UK) to submit poems for an anthology. I then accept one poem from everyone who has submitted, advising the poet in each instance that his poem is to appear in the anthology which may be purchased for, for argument's sake, £9.50. Effectively this means that each poet (if buying a copy of the anthology when invited to do so) has paid £9.50 *to have one poem published!*

Better still, there is a strong chance that many poets

included will buy copies for their friends and loved ones because they *have* been included – I invite them to do so. Go further – invite them to buy more than one copy with a once-and-only offer of a discounted, pre–publication price. "The anthology will cost the general public £12," I tell them as inducement.

Some months later I can send each poet a couple of pounds as 'royalties' and everyone is happy. Let us say that the anthology has cost me £3.75 a copy to produce, market and publicise. Each copy has sold for £9.50 and I have just sent each poet £2.35. That means that I have a profit level of £9.50 less £3.75, less £2.35 = £3.40 *per copy sold*.

It works as long as you have a large enough number of entrants and you're not too choosy what you accept as good enough to publish. Picking your subject areas must also be cleverly handled. If you were to publicise nationwide that you are to publish an anthology of poems by lefthanded greengrocers about plums, you'd get precious few entries! Publicise that you want poems for an anthology entitled *My Favourite Cat* and you'd be inundated with well written poems (a few) and utterly bilious, icky–sicky, poetical tripe (an immense number) for years. Finely organised you could even give a quite substantial prize for the best poem if you wished.

Yet every one in the past who tried it has found it fail in the end – you cannot be all things to all men. Sooner or later the good poets realised what was going on and dropped away and eventually the weak poets (who stood little chance of getting published elsewhere) got bored. Back in the late 50s/ early 60s it was rumoured that a company working this ploy, sharpened it a little by simply leaving out the poems from those (who'd been told they were 'in') if they hadn't bought a copy of the anthology – interesting.

But do any of the working practices mentioned in this chapter make vanity press of publishers? One or two of the publishers vanity press? None or some of them vanity press? That, reader, is something only *you* may decide.

Whatever you do decide though, there is an interesting game you may like to play – *spot the resurrection* . If you have decided that any one of the publishers in either list is vanity press, then make a note of the address and telephone number. If you find a new name appears in the advertising columns of the national press ignore the name, but compare the address, or even just the name of the town and certainly the telephone number.

All-in-all, if you cannot find a recognised poetry publisher to publish your poetry you would be better off self-publishing (see *Metric Feet & Other Gang Members*) and doing your own marketing, rather than paying somone else to do for you, what you may well be able to undertake just as well for yourself.

Marketing a poetry book is after all a completely different ball game, made no easier if you have initially parted with a large sum of money which you need to recoup before you even break even.

But, before we look at your possible market and the buying policies there, we should look at how publishers, and in some cases the individual, can be funded. However, there is a further facet of publishing which I feel bears some consideration and understanding before we move on.

I've always felt that if a poem was well written it didn't matter two kopecs who had written it, it deserved publishing, but many ethnic, and/or minority groups, have felt ill-used by the publishing world.

Women writers have for years felt themselves to be disadvantaged by the mainly male-dominated publishing world (disadvantaged not simply by the male macho: 'women belong in the kitchen and more important, subserviently in the bedroom', but something more fundamental than that – a sense of identity?) and so set up their own publishing houses.

I cannot envisage anyone *less* competent than I to comment on, or try to explain the need for, the female press, so I invited Peggy Poole – member of the Society of Women Writers and Journalists, Poetry Consultant to BBC Radio North West's *Write Now* and a fine poet in her own right – to enlarge on the need to be . . .

CHAPTER IV

WOMEN ONLY
by
Peggy Poole

The whole question of 'women only' groups, societies, publishers and publications has to be seen in a historical perspective. It is important to look back to the slow movement, mostly fought every inch of the way by men, to treat women as equals, important to remember laws that said a woman's inheritance or possessions belonged to her husband, or that she was the chattel of her father/husband/ brother. Laws which had to be changed.

Important too to recall the time when women were not considered fit to vote. The time when barriers against women being acceptable as degree students at either Cambridge or Oxford or as entrants to any medical college effectively stopped their entering the professions or becoming doctors. The way women were all-but banished from the work force after each of the two world wars was a powerful set-back, and the fight for equal pay for equal work is not yet universally won.

There has been a long conspiracy to keep women 'in their place'. Urgent necessity made George Eliot, Currer Bell et al use those gender-hiding pseudonyms.

Women were discriminated against in the field of sex, too; it took generations to squash the insistence that women neither needed nor were allowed to acknowledge enjoyment of intercourse. Which leads fairly consistently, to another important if not historical point, often overlooked. The experience of childbirth is dynamic; whereas men can gradually develop their own creative powers over the years, the majority of women suddenly have a huge chunk of their lives sliced out, when their personal creativity is entirely directed towards other dependent beings. Though the situation is much more fluid, it is still true, even in the

1990s, that females are the key carers of children and males the key bread-winners.

Quite apart from a loss of financial independence, this can also result in a terrifying loss of confidence in a woman, which surfaces when she is at last free to turn her mind to her own work. It is an area almost incomprehensible to men and one area where only other women can offer support.

On a personal note, I shall never forget the shock when, after years of looking after two daughters, I began to broadcast and *found people were prepared to pay for what I had to offer.* Many people still see women's writing as 'a little hobby for the wife' whereas husbands engaged in writing are 'men at work'. And no man can ever experience the humiliation of being a woman of 36+++ whose doctor sees any complaint only in terms of the menopause (and therefore hysteria) or old age (and therefore senility!).

Again, few men experience the corrosive 'guilt' syndrome. Some years ago I went to a christening where three highly intelligent women revealed how they were wrestling with guilt: the mother of the new Christian because this was her third child which meant she was adding to the problem of over-population; a second woman because she was wasting her undoubted talents by "only being a mum," and the third guest, a brilliant business-woman, because her children were left daily in charge of a nanny and could she be "depriving them of true maternal care?" Men are seldom in such 'no-win' situations.

Having at last escaped from the dependency of children, a woman frequently finds herself having to care for an infirm parent, her own or her husband's. She understands all too well how little personal space that hurrying chariot may allow her.

All of which adds up, it could be argued, to a case for treating women with extra consideration. Many have found it difficult to see themselves as *individuals* – not as daughter, wife, mother – let alone as serious writers. We have a lot of ground to make up. Which brings us to 'women only' organisations. Let's take the societies first.

A great many of the attitudes and strictures mentioned at the start of this chapter prevailed at the birth, in 1894, of *The Society of Women Writers and Journalists*. Some, in certain areas, still do.

When I suggested a fellow writer should join she said "Oh, but I'm not a feminist writer." (It is not only men who are prejudiced against women only groups!). The Society's members include, or have included, Vera Brittain, Joyce Grenfell, Clemence Dane, Rebecca West, Nina Bawden, Lady Longford – none of them noted feminists, none of their work in any way confined to female subjects. The Society does not get together to chat 'women' things as is sometimes alleged; family background is irrelevant and seldom touched on, but, as in other societies for specific groups, there is a high level of shared understanding which has a positive effect. We meet for lectures from eminent writers/editors – one of the first speakers was George Bernard Shaw – and we meet to talk of and advise each other about writing which, with members in any and every genre is consistently very helpful.

The need for such a body is borne out by the annual meeting when hundreds come together from all over the country. In 1993 I had an eye–opener as to the distance women still have to go before we are accepted by the general public for our talents in the way men are. When, before the formalities began, I left my case with the hall porter of one of London's big hotels, he asked: "Are you a W or a J?" Somewhat amused I replied "Well, I was once a J but am now more of a W." (I thought the introduction of a P would complicate the picture too much). "Oh" he smiled, the patronising tone of his voice strikingly evident "Have you ever had anything published?" "You cannot be a member of this Society," I answered very firmly, "unless you are a published writer." Clearly astonished he had hastily to adjust his attitude to the "gabble of women."

The Society's aims include "the encouragement of literary achievement, the upholding of professional standards, and social contact with other writers."[1] It is in no way exclusive nor is it a cosy coterie. It began as the "first of its kind to be run as an association of women engaged in journalism as writers or as artists in the United Kingdom, the Dominions, the Colonies and abroad"[1] – at that time the only professional women workers with no representative association. Such an organisation cannot suddenly turn its back on its original ethos because things have somewhat improved. And if you feel complacent about the position of women today, talk to some Asian girls living in Britain.

When I felt the need to belong to a professional body it was that historical background and that shared understanding which made me join the SWWJ and I have always felt it to be right for me.

Now we come to women only publishers and publications. Specialist publishers exist in many fields and, if amongst them there is felt to be a need exclusively to publish women writers, presumably market research has revealed such a need. The success of Virago has certainly justified their existence; they have become a highly respected house which has done an enormous amount to raise the low profile of neglected women writers and launch many of today's literary stars. The Onlywomen Press is very specific in its aims; authors feel comfortable to be under their umbrella because it immediately makes a statement; Radclyffe Hall might well have welcomed them in her day.

As far as poetry is concerned, I know the NPF has no bias – the ratio of collections by women compared to men slightly favours women – indeed the fact that Johnathon Clifford asked me to discuss the question of women only groups means he wants to get to grips with it. Nor are most editors of magazines prejudiced; I do not find Roger Elkin of *Envoi* in any way biased, he looks only for good poetry regardless of the poet's gender; as does David Holliday of

[1]quoted from SWWJ's current centenary leaflet.

107

Iota and Mike Shields of *Orbis*. There may still be a few editors who tend to look more favourably on the work of male poets than on their female counterparts, but that is as likely to be part of a subjective reaction to a poem as to any question of preferential treatment of one sex or the other. In choosing poems for BBC programmes, which I have done for many years, the background, age, professional qualifications, family situation or sex of the poet is totally immaterial. I am sure most editors share that approach.

Of course there are books of poetry only by women such as Faber's *20th Century Women's Poetry* edited by Fleur Adcock, Virago's *Book Of Wicked Verse* and Stride's *Frankenstein's Daughter*; there are also books of Caribbean Verse and Contemporary American Verse and books by disabled poets. This year I have edited, with Alison Chisholm, a collection of poems on apples and snakes. Experience showed us that – possibly because every woman has been burdened with Eve's guilt as seen by men – women feel compelled at some point to write an apple and/or snake poem. So rightly or wrongly we decided *Windfall*[2]should consist only of poems by women. In cases like these, it is not a question of wanting to be exclusive, but of having specific aims for the publication.

Apart from being included in anthologies with particular themes, I personally prefer that my work should compete without being defined, and perhaps confined, by sex, age or any other label. I have considerable reservations about poetry being boxed–in, mainly because there can be a down side. Prejudices immediately, even if subconsciously, come into play – expecting an all–women collection to be stridently feminist, sentimentally romantic or a special, minor genre, expecting Caribbean poetry to be full of rap, certainly not of the quality of *Omeros*, expecting poems from the disabled to be a cry for help – which means those books are either left on the shelf or are not read with a receptive mind.

[2]Published by Kettleshill Press, June 1994.

There is another danger too, in the possibility of such books being *sectioned off from poetry* in bookshops and libraries and put under separate categories of Women, Caribbean, and Health. Not so very long ago national newspapers introduced women's pages. This was a step forward in providing a platform for unknown journalists, as well as for people of the stature of Jill Tweedie and Mary Stott. These two in particular were enormously influential in enabling women to understand and improve the pattern of their lives, and thousands of us owe them a huge debt. But, conversely, men – whose minds might have been enlightened by such features – were often reluctant to be seen reading a Woman's Page. Today such articles are usually part of the paper as a whole which is as it should be.

Emily Dickinson had her Blue Peninsula – a land "of hope and dreamed delight"[3] where women can be themselves as men are themselves." If you are searching for a particular place you are not going to be given assistance from people who have no idea what you are seeking. The best directions come from those who have been there, who know exactly what you are looking for and why, and will even show you a short cut.

Vanity Press & The Proper Poetry Publishers deals specifically with poetry books, but the difficulties against which women poets have to battle are, of course, shared – possibly to a greater degree – by their counterparts in art and music. Writers can, like Jane Austen, hide pen and paper and pretend to be doing embroidery; you cannot hide a violin or cello (long thought to be 'unladylike') or a large canvas. And while the need for such secrecy may not be so apparent or important, the need to protect pages, instruments or canvas from a toddler's exploring hands can still be vital.

I would not define myself as a feminist but I am certainly sympathetic to feminism. And when I read that

[3]*Literary Women; The Great Writers* by Ellen Moers,
published by W H Allen 1977.

109

English departments in US universities are "obsessed with *gynocriticism* [my italics], (the study of women's literature) and the problems of women, minorities and persons of colour"[4], then I would lead any protest march to insist on recognition that women are part of the human race, not a race apart. In the long run this may only be achieved by like–minded people banding together.

[4]Review by Eric Anderson of *Battle Of The Books; The Curriculum Debate In America* by James Atlas. *The Sunday Telegraph* 6 March 1994.

CHAPTER V

It may well be the case that although you have found yourself a genuine publisher it is one which will still be hard pressed to cover the cost of your book. In this situation he may apply for grant aid to one of a number of bodies. You will note that I say "he." Most grant making bodies will entertain an application from a publisher though few a similar application from the poet. Grant making bodies will turn a deaf ear to anyone applying for a grant which involves a vanity publisher.

In the main the publisher should apply either to its Regional Arts Council or to its local Arts Association. In the following pages they each give you pointers to their rules for funding.

Clare Lynch, Literature Assistant for The **Eastern Arts Board**, Cherry Hinton Hall, Cherry Hinton Road, Cambridge CB1 4DW tel: 0223 215355, writes to tell me that they do give grants to publish poetry books. These are given to publishers and small presses in their own area. They also give bursaries to published poets to "buy time to write" but not to publish themselves. It would, she says, be unusual for them to offer more than £2,000 for a single publication, which would always be judged on literary merit. Their publication budget for 1994/95 is £23,000, a sizable proportion of which is committed to on-going clients and covers both Poetry and Literary Fiction.

Liza Pickard and Debbie Hicks are the people at the **East Midlands Arts** Literary Department, Mountfields House, Forest Road (entrance off Epinal Way), Loughborough, Leicestershire LE11 3HU tel: 0509 218292, to whom applications should be sent. In their general guidelines it

111

says that publishing funds are allocated by the Publishing Task Group which draws on specialist advisers in the field. "Literary excellence" is the over-riding consideration when giving a subsidy, though it isn't possible to apply a single set of literary values to every submission. It is up to the applicant in his editorial statement to make the context of the writing clear and show a good standard of production. Distribution and general administration are also important criteria.

The Publishing Task Group's first concern is with contemporary writing. Publication funds are awarded to small presses based in the region and occasionally to a publisher from another region where the work to be published is of especial advancement in the writer's career.

Support for self-publishing is not entertained, nor can an award be made 'in retrospect'. Applicants will be considered at a February/March meeting each year and a formal application form must be obtained and returned in time for consideration. In some cases an award may take the form of a 'guarantee against loss', up to 50% may be paid in advance where necessary.

Jean Dupre for The **London Arts Board**, Elme House, 133 Long Acre, Covent Garden, London WC2E 9AF tel: 071 240 1313 tells me they are to introduce a new award later this year (1994) in the form of three bursaries of £3,500 each to London writers of a first book of fiction or poetry who need to "buy time" to complete a second book. Writers can be of any nationality as long as they are resident in London, must have published *no more than* one book of fiction or one full length collection of poetry (pamphlets don't count) and must show evidence of work-in-progress, a need for financial assistance and a plan for how the bursary would be used. For an entry form apply to *New London Writers' Awards*, address above.

Publishers or poets may apply to John Bradshaw (Head of Published and Broadcast Arts) **Northern Arts**, 9–10 Osborne Terrace, Jesmond, Newcastle Upon Tyne NE2 1NZ tel: 091 281 6334, for financial support if they live in Cleveland, Cumbria, Durham, Northumberland or Tyne & Wear. An application form must be accompanied by a copy of, or extracts from, the manuscript to be published. All publications must be produced to a high standard, and adequate plans for promotion, distribution and sales must be included with any application.

From the Literature Department of **North West Arts**, 12 Harter Street, Manchester M1 6HY tel: 061 228 3062, either Marc Collett or Christine Bridgwood will send you an application form. Their publishing grants scheme offers financial assistance to small press and community publishers to publish, market and distribute writing by north west writers. Any small press based in the north west region may apply. Publishers based outside the region may apply if the proposed publication is by a writer who lives in the north west region. Publishers based in the region but producing a publication from outside the region as a part of a long–term publishing programme may also apply. "Vanity presses" where a financial contribution is required from the author as a condition of publication are not eligible to apply, nor are self–publishers or publishers who do not intend to make a charge for the publication.

Sue Robertson, Executive Director, for **Southern Arts**,13 St Clement Street, Winchester, Hants SO23 9DQ tel: 0962 855099, writes to tell me of their support for poetry – it is a shame that my book is specifically about poetry books, for it would appear that Southern Arts spent some £54,000 in support of poetry (everything from bursaries through prizes to workshops). Supported 2 Russian poets in 1993

113

and 3 Polish poets in 1994, residencies and *Writers in Education* and a Library service.

Where poetry presses are concerned they subsidised 4 in 1993: *Illuminations*, the Isle of Wight; *Phoenix Press* in Berkshire; *The Haiku Quarterly* in Wiltshire and *KQBX* of Dorset – a total of £3,000.

As from April of '94 their Literary Officer is to be Keiren Phelan, to whom enquiries relating to publication grants should be sent in the first instance.

Mark Homer, Literary Development Officer for **Surrey Arts** on behalf of **South East Arts**, 10 Mount Ephraim, Tunbridge Wells, Kent TN4 8AS tel: 0892 515210, told me that Celia Hunt is their Literary Officer, and faxed me information on their *Writers Bursaries* (total budget £6,000) under which there are a number of awards of £1,000–£2,000. Applications are invited from writers who are in the early stages of their careers and who have had a number of poems or stories published in journals, magazines or anthologies and who need to "buy time" on a specific project – whether to cover a period of unpaid leave, cost of childcare or help with costs of a period of writing in residence at a retreat.

Their *Training Bursaries* (total budget £1,000) in awards of £100–£200 are open to published or unpublished writers who have done a certain amount of work but who need funding to attend residential writing courses such as those run by Arvon or Fen.

These awards are open to those living in the South East Arts region of Kent, Surrey, East and West Sussex and those interested should apply initially for an application form to Rachel Donnelly, Administrative Assistant, Media and Published Arts Unit, South East Arts.

Ingrid Squirrell, Literary Officer for **South West Arts**, Bradninch Place, Gandy Street, Exeter EX4 3LS tel: 0392 218188, wrote to tell me that they do give grants to publish poetry books, to smaller presses to publish mainly books by individuals, but sometimes by groups. They support 3 or 4 such presses which publish about 24 books a year. The criteria for support is quality of material, of production, of marketing, publicity and financial planning. There is no minimum/maximum to grant levels but only those running a press may apply.

Sally Luton, Director of Management Services for **West Midlands Arts**, 83 Granville Street, Birmingham B1 2LH tel: 021 631 3121, faxed me to say that West Midlands Arts offers finance for the publishing of new literary work, including poetry, through a *New Work and Production Awards Scheme*.

Awards are usually made to the publisher or editor to cover the commissioning fee/s of contributors and may contribute to production costs. The awards are not available to support vanity publishers, or, with the rare exception, self–publishing.

Funds available for the award scheme during 1994/95 are limited and amount to £10,000 for all aspects of literature. Anyone wishing to apply should first contact the Information Officer on 021 624 3200 (direct line) and are strongly advised to contact the Literary Officer, David Hart to talk through their plans. Messages may be left for him with Pauline Pearson the Administrative Assistant.

The Literary Officer for **Yorkshire & Humberside Arts**, 21 Bond Street, Dewsbury, Yorkshire WF13 1AX tel: 0924 455555, Jill Leahy, sent me details of their *Literature Publication Award Scheme* 1994/5 and their Broadcast & Published Arts Summary 1994/95. They administer *New*

Beginnings: Writers Awards which offers 4 grants of up to £1,500 each to enable writers to concentrate on specific writing projects. *Literature Publication Awards Scheme* is designed to support a wide range of publications, with a preference given to imaginative writing. The total amount available for this award scheme is £10,000. In the brochure for this scheme it states that that they will only offer support for publication where the publisher or author are based in the region, that they do not fund 'local history' and that "applicants from vanity presses where the author is self–publishing or where a financial contribution either in cash or through purchase of a certain number of copies is required from the author as a condition of publication, cannot be considered." Applicants may request support in either the form of a loan or grant. Two copies of the manuscript in question must accompany any application.

* * *

Dr Alastair Niven, Director of Literature for the **Arts Council of England**,14 Great Peter Street, London SW1P 3NQ tel: 071 333 0100, writes that they fund both Anvil Press (£61,600 in 94/95) and Carcanet (£67,800 for the same period). The former is entirely a poetry press, the latter with a substantial poetry list. Anvil publishes some 15 poetry titles a year, Carcanet 30. They also fund journals where poetry and poetry debate appear side by side: *Ambit* (£8,740); *PN Review* (£17,580) and *Poetry Review* (funded from within the Poetry Society's grant). Other journals include *London Review of Books* (£27,640), *London Magazine* (£23,000) and *Wasafiri* (£7,000) – all these are 'clients'. In addition approximately 20 books of poetry in translation are supported each year (£100,000, plus up to £10,000 extra supplied by the British Council). A total of some 65 poetry books a year.

116

Grants are normally given to the publishers, but the Council always ask to see the contract between publisher and author. Self–publishing is not normally supported.

The Council aims to support quality of both writing and the design of the product, but applicants must also show a reasonable means of distribution and give a platform to writers whose work might not otherwise be published.

The Arts Council also provide at least 15 annual Writers' Awards of £7,000 each, funds the Poetry Society (£147,800) and the Poetry Book Society (£48,600), apart from additional initiatives such as the Libretti fund and Cultural Diversity budget.

For The **Arts Council of Northern Ireland**, 185 Stranmillis Road, Belfast BT9 5DU tel: 0232 381591, Ciaron Carson, Literature Editor, told me that until recently they have had a committee that sat in September and February each year to consider applications for grant aid. Everything is now very much in flux but they are shortly to have an Arts Council Board which will sit much more often. He said that he was very much against the vanity press and that they wouldn't support such projects.

Walter Cairns, Literature Director of the **Scottish Arts Council**, 12 Manor Place, Edinburgh, Scotland EH3 7DD tel: 031 226 6051, tells me that they give between 90 and 100 grants a year to publishers of which perhaps a third are for poetry anthologies or books about poetry or poets. He told me that they never consider giving a grant to an author, only the publisher. Nor would they *ever* consider funding a vanity press. Although they used to support publishers in England who were to publish something of particular interest to Scotland, due to the tightening up of finances they can now only support presses actually based in Scotland. They have a complimentary backup service to anything that is published in Scotland which is organised by Tessa Ransford, Librarian at the Scottish Poetry Library, Tweeddale Court, 14 High Street, Edinburgh EH1 1TE tel: 031 557 2876. There is a Catalogue of the Lending Collection of the Library, a Membership Scheme, a Poetry Library Newsletter and automatic cataloguing and subject-indexing system, INSPIRE, designed by Gordon Dunsire of Napier Polytechnic, Edinburgh in co-operation with staff at the Scottish Poetry Library – you'll need an IBM-compatible PC with DOS (version 3.1 or higher) to benefit from this.

Angela Howells, of the Literary Department of **The Arts Council of Wales**, Museum Place, Cardiff, Wales CF1 3NX tel: 0222 394711, sent me a leaflet entitled *Production Grants To Publishers*. It should be noted that up until recently each region in Wales had a separate Arts Council, but now each of the old regional arts councils have become local offices of the central Arts Council in Cardiff and all publishers looking for grant aid have to apply to this body.

Applications are considered by the *Grants To Publishers* Panel twice a year. The publisher must provide detailed estimates of the book production for which he is claiming on the forms available from the Council Offices. There is a fee of £20 for each typescript up to 200 pages and a £30 fee for typescripts with over 200 pages. Submissions have to be accompanied by the correct fee. The typescript – which will be sent to one or two readers with a knowledge of poetry who will normally be paid a £20-£40 reading fee – must not bear the name of the author, though his name should be made known to the Literature Department, the officers of which are always willing to offer advice. The readers are chosen from outside the membership of the Literature Board. It is their duty to recommend whether or not the Arts Council of Wales should be associated with the project and a copy of their report will be sent to the publisher.

No application will be considered retrospectively nor will the Council subsidise vanity publishing.

Welsh language publishers resident in Wales are more likely to receive grant aid from The **Welsh Books Council**, Castell Brychan, Aberystwyth, Dyfed SY23 1JB tel: 0970 624151 who, their Director Miss Gwefyl Pierce Jones tells me, are themselves funded by local authorities and the Welsh Office. They not only hold (in 1994) a £600,000 budget specifically for the support of Welsh language books and magazines, but also supply general services of design, marketing and distribution, and hold a stock of some 4,000 titles, half of which are Welsh language.

CHAPTER VI

The problem with marketing the book of an unknown poet is that in the accepted sense of the word 'marketing' it is extremely difficult if not impossible.

There's always the chance that if you can interest newspapers and radio in the poet's backyard to give the book coverage you'll stand a chance of persuading local bookshops to take a few copies on the strength of the publicity the book is to attract. But invariably they will need some convincing to pay for them 'up front', much preferring to take copies only on on a sale or return basis, which would be all very well if it wasn't for the fact that half what you get back are then 'seconds' – no longer saleable for the full cover price – and it ties up your stock copies. Much better to try and get local bookshops to buy them, though you're sure to have to offer a minimum of a third discount to entice them to do so.

There's family and friends – normally the largest sales outlet – but here the poet has to beware of pressure to *give* copies away. Auntie will expect one as her right – so will unc' and bro' and sis' and . . . the 'free' list can get endless if you allow it. All must be made to understand that the book has cost hard money to produce and the poet, adopting a hard–hearted stance, hold out for the full cover price; Auntie's convincing tales of personal hardship not withstanding! Of course, more often than not the poet feels uncomfortable or embarrassed at having to ask members of the family to pay up, and so – red–faced and clothed in nothing but confusion – gives away copy after copy to everyone who asks.

"But what," you will ask, "of the expansive promises by the publisher to market my book for me?" The genuine publisher will make an effort to do so and have the contacts to make it possible, but much of the promised help with sales and associated 'royalties' may prove far less valuable and helpful than first appeared to be the case.

You'll find that most publishers will offer to publish a set number of copies for you. Not a number that has been arrived at randomly or by accident either, but a number that has normally been found to be moveable – with a bit of hard work on your own part. Don't forget, we are here talking of you the unknown poet published by a small press or even (dare we say it) a vanity press, rather than a well known poet published by a company with promotional clout.

With a genuine publisher the number published will lend itself to being sold at a sensible price – if you are to have 200 copies of a 40 page booklet published for £3,000 it is obvious that each book must sell for £15 for you to even break even. But no 40 page book is worth more than £5 a copy unless a *very* special production. Most would be left on your shelf. The number published must be cost effective against size of book and price to be charged.

If you are an unknown poet, recognise yourself as being simply that and accept the fact that, whatever you are told, unless you have a large supportive family and a simply huge number of friends you will be lucky to clear 100 copies as a minimum and 300 at most. Promises of large sales by the publisher as a result of his own 'marketing' rarely materialise.

But what of your possible market – the bookshops and library suppliers? How do they approach the buying of poetry books? The following list, apart from containing the major players in the market, also includes a random selection of the smaller bookshops. When I wrote to each I also (to substantiate the claims of the advertising publishers) sent my list on page 52 and asked whether they bought poetry books from any of these companies.

A.

Anthony Zurbrugg, Manager for the **Africa Book Centre**, 38 King Street, Covent Garden, London WC2E 8JT tel: 071 240 6649, writes that they carry a big selection of African writers. What they carry depends on quality and availability. 98% of their stock is in English, but they do also carry French, Somali, Hausa, Yoruba, and Swahili titles and normally stock some 100 poetry books. They produce general flyers which include both prose and poetry but would produce a poetry-only list if it was felt necessary and someone was prepared to pay them to do so. They have a thriving mail order business.

Alex Bennet and his wife own the **Amberstone Bookshop** at 49 Upper Orwell Street, Ipswich, Suffolk IP4 1HP tel: 0473 250675. Alex tells me they stock between 40 and 50 poetry books – the major classical poets and those which are titles used by students at the Suffolk College. He feels less poetry is sold these days. "People used to come in and buy the First World War poets, but don't so much now, for instance," he said. Where the vanity press are concerned he stressed that although some local people had come in with books they had published that way, he'd only take what he had an order for.

B.

Karen George, Marketing Manager for **Blackwell Retail Ltd**, 8 Broad Street, Oxford OX1 3AJ tel: 0865 792792, writes that they do buy books from the listed publishers (but does not say how many poetry books as a percentage of the total) and believe in experimenting – taking orders on the basis of quality of the specific title/s and often taking pamphlets containing poems produced by the poet and other privately published magazines. They normally buy on a sale or return basis – there would need to be a very good reason to order on a 'firm sale' basis – and expect discounts of between 35%–45%. She says they encourage carrying small press books where appropriate. Their shops buy individually though she may undertake a central poetry promotion to secure good branded point of sales and better terms. She does not dictate the stock holding of individual shops. Information is sent out in the form of a monthly Blackwell's Marketing Update which carries all publicity information both generic and publisher specific. She will send out information about a book 'making the news' as long as she knows about it in plenty of time. "As for prizes," she wrote, "we support local prizes and may look at one of our own in the future."

Anne and Philip Jowett own and run **The Bookshop**, High Street, Cranley, Surrey GU6 8AZ tel: 0483 274265. Anne tells me they buy local poets normally through the poet coming into the shop with their book. The only other poetry they carry is the well established poets they know will sell which they buy through catalogues rather than from reps.

Alan and Joan Tucker own and run **The Bookshop**, Station Road, Stroud, Gloucester GL5 3AP tel: 0453 764736. Alan tells me that they have a larger poetry section than most. Apart from stocking the established poet they buy good, lesser known poets and try wherever possible to cater for the requirements of their clients. When asked, he said that he wouldn't waste his time with vanity press reps.

C.

Yvonne Sharp, owner of **Chipping Campden Bookshop**, Dragon House, High Street, Chipping Campden, Gloucestershire GL55 6AG tel; 0386 840944, told me that although they are very small she "wouldn't feel she was a serious bookshop if she didn't stock poetry books." Apart from getting in books against special order, she also stocks titles for which she believes she may find a market. These she buys through the representatives from reputable publishers. She says she never sees reps from any of the vanity press.

D.

Manager Christine Shearer for **Deptford Bookshop and Literacy Centre**, 55 Deptford High Street, London SE8 4AA tel: 081 691 8339, tells me that they carry mainly Children's dual language books in English/Vietnamese, English/Punjabi, English/Urdu, English/Gujarati, English/Bengali and English/Somali, but that they do occasionally carry Black poetry on a sale or return basis.

Helen Thomas, Purchasing Manager for **Dillons The Bookstore**, Berwick House, 35 Livery Street, Birmingham B3 2PB tel: 021 236 6886, wrote that all their stores are independent and purchase their own stock. When an account is opened (through her at head office) she agrees terms and payment methods, which information is then passed to all the stores.

She said that they did not have accounts with Merlin Books, Avon Books or Minerva Press, but that they did have accounts with the others on the list. "Stores may only order books from those with whom we do have an account," she writes.

E.

Margaret Dunne for **W H Everett & Sons Ltd**, 8 Hurlingham Business Park, Sulivan Road, London SW6 3DU tel: 071 731 8562, told me their main customers are University Libraries abroad and that the weight of their business is export, though they will supply to the home market where requested. They also supply to Government Agencies, Industry and Booksellers world wide. Everetts buy in against firm order – most of their customers knowing exactly what they want – but also give a bibliographic service where requested, to up–date clients on the availability of the latest publications.

F.

Robert Hawthorn, Assistant Stock Manager of **T C Farries and Co Ltd**, Irongray Road, Lochside, Dumfries, Scotland DG2 0LH tel: 0387 720755, rang to tell me that they are Library Suppliers. They have a policy where a person with a specific interest in a subject is put in charge of buying. Thus the poetry buyer has a particular interest in poetry. Farries have a 'static collection' as an exhibition for their customers and also a fleet of mobile vans which tour the country on a weekly basis taking new publications to the libraries. They obviously stock the established poets, but also provide books to order, stock local poets (Borders and Scotland) and at the same time give an up to the moment service of new books available, to their customers.

A name which is synonymous with 'bookshop', **W and G Foyle Ltd**, 113–119 Charing Cross Road, London WC2H 0EB tel: 071 437 5660, were sent in December 1993 (along with every other book shop) a copy of a standard questionnaire addressed to the poetry book buyer. Having not received a reply I wrote again . . . twice in the course of 6 weeks . . . still no reply. I wrote recorded delivery to their Managing Director – no reply. In mid March Eileen Murray went into Foyles on my behalf. She was shown up to see their Poetry Buyer, Steven Boal. He apparently agreed that he had a copy of one of my letters, and (she told me) said that the reason I hadn't received a reply was

THE OXFORD COMPANION TO TWENTIETH-CENTURY POETRY

edited by
Ian Hamilton

An alphabetically arranged history of modern poetry, covering its development across the whole of the English-speaking world.

Covers 1,500 poets from Abse to Zaturenska as well as magazines, movements, critical terms and concepts from the beginning of the century to the present day.

Entries provide bibliographical data on poets' published work and major biographical and critical works on them.

A select bibliography of anthologies supplies a handy source of information on poets whose work is not otherwise in print or readily available to readers.

Full details from The Oxford University Press, Order department, FREEPOST NH 4051, Corby, Northants NN18 9BR tel: 0536 741519.

Ian Hamilton is a distinguished poet and biographer. The former editor of several literary magazines including *The New Review* and *Times Literary Supplement*, he presented the Bookmark series for BBC TV.

because at Foyles they were all so 'laid back', but that I would get an answer. I haven't.

It would have been helpful to have received an answer from Foyles about their poetry book buying policies but as Eileen sold Steven four copies of her own book *Simple Seasons* (NPF Publications, ISBN 1 870556 28 3) while there I can confirm Foyles do buy poetry books. I can also confirm that as their telephone number (unlike any other literary company in the UK), is no more than an answering machine on which you cannot leave a message, for "they are too busy to take calls," there's no satisfaction to be gained by ringing.

If it is a fact that Mr Boal et al are so 'laid back', it is fortunate I was not some house-bound invalid trying to order a special book for say, some loved-one's birthday present. She *would* have been so desperately disappointed!

H.

Andrew Sharp, Literary Department Manager for **Heffers Booksellers**, 20 Trinity Street, Cambridge CB2 3NG tel: 0223 358351, told me that they not only look at poetry book lists from all the major publishers both in the UK and abroad but also from Password. They like to buy from local authors, usually on a sale or return basis, though they are flexible. They have a 'children's bookclub' entitled *Bookworm* and also supply to libraries. They look for a minimum 40% discount from all suppliers. They do not see reps on spec, but an appointment has to be made in advance.

Tom Lee for **Holt Jackson Books Ltd**, Preston Road, Lytham, Lancs FY8 5AX tel: 0253 737464, says that they order poetry books for libraries, take them 'on approval' and also set up static poetry book displays for their area libraries. They wouldn't buy vanity press books.

J.

Pat Darby, Purchasing Manager of **JMLS Ltd**, 24 Gamble Street, Nottingham NG7 4FJ tel: 0602 708021, rang to tell me that their aim is to promote the broadest range of titles possible to their customers. To this end they ask publishers to up-date them continually with information about forthcoming publications, which in turn is entered on a database which is available either in house, or by a 'lital system' to customers who can link into this database through a computer. There is also a weekly 'forthcoming books' list circulated to customers which contains as much information as possible.

Where individual books are concerned, if JMLS buyers decide that there is a title they wish to hold as 'approval stock', they ask the publisher concerned to send them a minimum of 60 copies on a sale or return basis. These are sent 'on approval' to libraries.

Obviously many poetry publishers are in the small press league; unable to afford to off-load so many books on a sale or return basis; but still, by sending as much information as possible about each publication, even the smallest of publishers can have their publications databased and included on the JMLS weekly 'forthcoming books' list. Should JMLS decide to carry a particular title as a stock item they would then buy in 5 or 6 copies.

Pat confirmed that she recognised most of the publishers on the list I read through to her, and that JMLS had bought books from many of them in the past.

O.

Peter Finch, Head of Bookshop for **Oriel**, The Friary, Cardiff CF1 4AA tel: 0222 395548, tells me Oriel have a brief to stock a wide range of poetry by living poets "from all over" and that they reckon to have the widest selection of poetry anywhere outside London. He goes on to say that

PASSWORD

Password offers a complete representation and distribution service, including sales representation, order processing, customer liaison, invoicing, storage and despatch of books (including insurance), issuing of statements, credit control and cash collection. Payments are then paid to publishers monthly with reports of sales and stock levels. The company subcontracts the 'physical' aspects of distribution: storage, picking, packing and despatching of books, while retaining overall control and responsibility for the process.

For the complete service described above, Password charges 30% of net sales plus VAT. Commission is based on net invoice value, i.e. after discount which is usually 35%.

Password also runs training courses for small publishers. Please phone for a brochure.

For full details contact: David Parrish, Managing Director, Password, 23 New Mount Street, Manchester M4 4DE tel: 061 953 4009.

* * *

"Stockwell send us covers when they have a local author; Book Guild now and again send us jackets; the others never." They will always buy local authors no matter how their titles are originated although "we always order less from vanity sources," he states.

"In a perfect world," he writes, "good poetry would outsell the bad but this is not a perfect world. The hyped outsells the lesser known quality material. The big presses stand a better chance than the small." He feels that probably the best way for small presses to sell are hand to hand, or by direct mail, or any other way where they are not in direct competition with the likes of Faber & Faber or Bloodaxe.

"It is impossible to promote all poets equally. Someone must always come top, or first, or have their jacket facing the door or next to the till or whatever. We are in business to help poets and we do our best. A part of our profit margin is put towards helping the lesser knowns."

P.

For **Perbertons**, 4 High Town, Hay-On-Wye, Hereford HR3 5AE tel: 0497 820159, Diana Blunt tells me that although they are a very small bookshop and that there is already a poetry book shop in Wye, they do stock standard poetry books and also the Welsh poets for the Hay-On--Wye Festival at the end of May. They're more inclined to carry poetry books on a sale or return basis although they do buy from the likes of Faber & Faber and against firm customer order.

Kate Ballantyne, owner of **The Picture Book**, 1 The Gallery, Ashbourne, Derbyshire DE6 1MM tel: 0335 344008, tells me that she stocks mainly established poets – R S Thomas and Bloodaxe New Poetry were two she mentioned – and usually orders from wholesalers. She says she has never been approached by vanity press reps and wouldn't buy from them were she to be. "In my area I have to carry recognised 'names' where poetry is concerned, though I will get in special orders," she said.

Alan Halsey, owner of **The Poetry Bookshop**, 22 Broad Street, Hay-On-Wye, Herfordshire HR3 5DB tel: 0497 820305, tells me that he deals almost exclusively in second hand poetry books these days (98% of his business) and that he only really buys poetry books through a network of those he knows and with whom he has built up a relationship over the years. The only distributor with whom he deals is the Welsh Book Council. Of the list of publishers he says that Merlin send him flyers for books, often claiming the author to have won some prize or other, which he puts in the bin. Stockwells also occasionally send him flyers. He hasn't received anything from any of the others.

S.

Steve Hougham, RMD Books for **W H Smith Ltd**, Retail, Greenbridge Road, Swindon SN3 3LD tel 0793 616161, was helpful enough to send me a "statement of my position on submissions," dated 30th March 1994.

"Most importantly," he states, "I am happy to receive submissions for poetry books, at *any* time and from *any* source. However in the past 5 months that I have been the poetry buyer for W H Smith Ltd, I have not seen a submission from any of the publishers that you listed."

"In general, buying decisions are made approximately 3 months prior to publication date, but this does not exclude books that are submitted late for any reason."

"Any publisher, whether large or small, is welcome to arrange to see a particular buyer in person, or to write to W H Smith. Naturally we see all the major publishers on a regular monthly basis, but this is not to the exclusion of other suppliers. In fact, I frequently receive written submissions from many members of the public who have no formal representative."

"Wherever possible I need to see a finished copy of the book that I am buying. When this is not available, I usually request to see *at least* a manuscript and artwork for the jacket. I try to bring together as many sources of information as possible when buying any book. I frequently follow up postal submissions by requesting much more detailed information."

"My aim in choosing books is to present a balanced range of the best books available. This means good value for money, good quality of production and excellent content. Of course my choice *must* be profitable, and all our ranges do have a finite amount of space. There is no point in buying more books than we have space in which to display them."

"Poetry is undoubtedly a highly over–published sector of the book market, and this makes the number of success stories relatively small. To put this in context there are at least 10 times the amount of books published every year, than we have space to stock in our branches. Over--publishing is probably the biggest factor that reduces the chance of a book being sold at W H Smith, *not* our submission practices."

The **Strathtay Bookshop**, 8 Dunkeld Street, Aberfeldy, Perthshire, Scotland PH15 2DA tel: 0887 829519, is owned and run by Theresa and Barry Dunford. Theresa told me that though they find poetry normally sells very slowly they do buy both local and established poets. They would normally expect to buy on a 'sale or return' basis and to be offered around a 35% discount. She said that she hadn't, to her knowledge, ever been approached by a vanity   press   representative.

T.

For **James Thin Ltd** (until recently Melvens Bookshop), 29 Union Street, Inverness, Scotland IV1 1QA tel: 0463 233500, the Manager, Malcolm Herron, tells me they normally only obtain books against firm orders though they might take local poets' work. He added that he seldom heard from any of the vanity press and if he were to he would definitely only order against a firm customer request.

Marius Jociejowski, Manager for **The Turret Bookshop**, 36 Great Queen Street, London WC2B 5AA tel: 071 405 6058, writes that they try to "have a complete stock of poetry" and support those people who come in with a pamphlet they have published themselves, taking them on a sale or return basis. They also order poetry books to order. He says that they "avoid the vanity press although, quite honestly, we are rarely offered these."

W.

On behalf of **Waterstones**, Capital Court, Capital Interchange Way, Brentford, Middlesex TW8 0EX tel: 081 742 3800, Sales Development Manager, Nick Rennison, writes to tell me that, "of the publishers you mention we have accounts with all but three (Quest Publishing, Godfrey and Avon Books) although none is a large account. I do not receive books or covers from any of the publishers concerned and I think it unlikely that any of the shops do."

"I agree that Waterstones' poetry sections should include books from a wide range of poets and publishers and that the quality of the poetry should be a consideration when the buyer is making his or her buying decisions. I am sure that in the majority of our shops this is the case."

"I agree that Waterstones is an important means by

which poetry is brought to the public's attention and that our shops should carry titles from a wide range of quality poets. I think that the majority of our shops do."

"In most of our shops the poetry sections are larger and stock more books than purely commercial considerations would dictate. In this sense we already do our part in furthering poetry as an art form."

"I would dispute, for reasons apparent from my previous remarks, that the present situation in our shops is one which does little other than help large publishers or the already famous to promote their poetry irrespective of its merits."

"I acknowledge that poets published by the larger firms (eg Faber) are likely to get greater exposure than those published by smaller firms. I hope that Waterstones will continue to do its part in balancing the equation by carrying and displaying the work of good poets from a wide range of publishers."

* * *

Well there we have it. All the 'it' I was able to glean. I wouldn't claim for one minute that it is a complete and total picture, only that there is enough – from all those who have put themselves out to give me useful data – to draw an overall picture of the poetry book publishing situation in the UK today. What conclusions all this leads you to can only be yours – your personal appreciation of what is on offer, judged against what you feel you need. I can only say that it has been immense fun putting it all together and hope that you find it useful and, after you have become that lauded–in–the–past poet of great fame (and no fortune), who finds himself re–forgotten, you will need no more than . . . well . . . the facing page!

TWIGGERS

11 Fairmead Road
Shinfield
Reading RG2 9DL
tel: 0734 882001

Secondhand And Out–of–Print
BOOK FINDING SERVICE

Ordinary Book Search: This service is free for up to 4 titles per customer. Apply to the address below for the necessary form with an sae. We will automatically advertise once through trade journals to try to locate the book you require. If you have not heard within a month it means we have been unsuccessful.

Extended Search: We can carry out this search by advertising in trade journals for a search period of up to 4 months. This vastly increases the chances of locating the item required. The fee for this service is £2.50 per title.

US Search: We will also advertise in America for out––of–print titles not found in this country. The fee for this service is £2.50 per title.

We will inform you *only* when the title has been located, sending a full description of the condition of the book and the price, which includes postage. There is *no obligation to buy* as the eventual cost of each book can only be determined once it has been traced. As a guide we can say that the minimum cost to you for each title will not be less than £7.00.

INDEX
SPECIALIST PUBLISHERS

Languages separated by / indicates by the same publisher.